[TH THE
SCOTS 1054 - 1654

by

Gregory Lauder-Frost

**With a Foreword by
Henry von Blumenthal**

LONGCROSS PRESS

ISBN   978-99959-54-05-5

CAMPAIGNING WITH THE SCOTS 1054 - 1654

by

Gregory MacLennan Lauder-Frost,
B.A.(Hons), F.S.A. Scot.

with a Foreword by
Henry von Blumenthal

CONTENTS

Dedication

*I dedicate this book to the memory
of my beloved Grandfather,*

Matthew Currie Lauder (1899-1972)

*who served in both World Wars,
and to the memory of our ancestors
whose first loyalty was
always to King and Country.*

Foreword

Such political and military significance as the celebrated alliance between the French and Scots may have had did not always extend to cultural and linguistic ties, and, some would argue, had little effect on the social organisation of Scotland.

In this, as in the language, strong links can instead be found with Germany. In particular, it is striking what a close affinity there was between the ruling military classes of Scotland, bolstered by complex but closely monitored family ties, and the Junker society of Brandenburg and Pomerania. Two key similarities stand out.

In both societies, particular families would remain attached to their estates by law and custom, provision being made for younger sons so that cadet branches of families assumed an importance not well understood by the English who were accustomed to an elder-son--takes-all primogeniture.

In both societies, it was unthinkable that any male should not in the ordinary course of events be called upon to fight.

Such a system has its weaknesses. It could only work if the personal ambitions of individuals were subordinated to an acceptance of their place in the social order, with both its privileges and its dangers. The possibility of constant territorial squabbling which beset the cattle-rustling and mosstrooping periods of both societies, however, gave rise of necessity to codes of conduct which even now are proverbial. Above all, the martial qualities of duty, loyalty, and natural leadership became paramount.

The villains of Mr. Lauder-Frost's story, then, are those who betrayed the trust of those to whom they owed a natural and inherited duty, namely the Kings of Scotland. The heroes, the Lauders, are merely typical representatives of a much wider class of men who sought nothing for themselves but the satisfaction of knowing that they had passed their inheritance, not only of property, but also of honour, to their children intact.

Perhaps the one word which sums up this code of practice best is chivalry. It is no accident that it should have been a Scotsman, Sir Walter Scott, who revived this concept and illustrated it with stories from Scottish History. Later writers on the theme such as Kenelm Digby came to regard chivalry as an ideal to which anyone could aspire.

I do not think they are wrong. If more people, in whatever circumstances, were to look into the achievements and failures of their ancestors, they might find it easier to take pride in the achievements and to avoid the failings in their own lives. Mr Lauder-Frost therefore renders a double service: he has not only provided a useful insight into the vagaries of Scottish clan history, seen through the eyes of his family. He has also given an example of how it is possible for one family to stand up for a set of principles over many generations.

Henry von Blumenthal
Lameschmillen
Luxemburg, June 25 2018

INTRODUCTION

In writing this book I have attempted two things. The first is to acquaint the reader with a summary of some of the notable battles and skirmishes that the warriors of Scotland were involved in between 1054 and the great British Civil War. Because many of the standard history books so often only refer to the most senior people in command, I felt it necessary to comment on the broader nobility involved in the wars and intrigues. Often it was the minor barons and their commands who would make or break a battle rather than the overall commanders who seem to get all the mentions in history books.

In 1054 the Scottish nobility was minute (the entire population is estimated to have been only in the hundreds of thousands) and the only titles worth noting here were *Thanes,* originally a Scandinavian or Norse title, and the local magnates, the *Mormaers*, both of which were later converted to that of Earl. When Malcolm Canmore's forces came to Scotland in pursuit of Macbeth, they included contingents of Normans (notwithstanding the fact that the Norman Conquest of England did not occur for another 12 years) and some argue that this was the beginning of the introduction of the feudal system to Scotland. (Canmore's future wife, St.Margaret, had also been brought up and educated at Court in Hungary and was responsible for the introduction of many European ideas.)

Under the feudal system many titles and all lands were reversionary to the Crown. In the case of feudal baronies and other hereditary landholdings, this reversion usually happened upon death and marriage, so that in the new or re-grant of the barony or lands it was confirmed to a baron or *laird* and his heirs upon certain undertakings, which nearly always involved some kind of entry payment and/or service by the heir when his time came. Once this happened the King would confirm the charter. Under the feudal system all barons and the larger lairds could be called upon to provide men, provisions etc., for war from their respective lands. Many abused this power, raising men for their private armies in a vast variety of bids for power, or simply faction fighting. And many did not, remaining constantly loyal to their legitimate sovereign.

Heinrich von Treitschke, writing in *Freedom* said that "A State which allows its citizens to look after districts and communities in honorary service, gains moral force" and whilst he was writing in the 19th. Century, the ideal was part of the framework of the feudal system. Many barons founded schools, relieved the poor, cared for the aged and built hospitals.

Scotland's history is riddled with treachery. Many, it seems, were power mad, and the result was one conspiracy after another. One decade your neighbour was your friend, the next your sworn enemy as each moved from faction to faction. Treitschke, again, said that "reciprocal rights and duties connect the state with its citizens. But reciprocity is unthinkable between entities which are related to one another simply as means and object". Unfortunately for Scotland, the latter was the rule rather than the exception.

During the reigns of the last Stewarts more and more senior aristocratic titles were created for people who had never or rarely fought in the field, were often corrupt and sometimes anything but aristocratic and, as time passed, often held no territory. Successive Kings of the Scots saw the bestowing of titles as a means of buying loyalty.

There is little evidence that this system brought the monarchs much joy. My research has shown me that more than often people of considerable rank were, in fact, out and out traitors. The bribery and corruption that went on amongst some of these people, particularly in the century of the English Civil War (which eventually spread to Scotland and Ireland), is well recorded. Many historians argue that the 17th century corruption was the nail in the coffin that led to the extinction of Scotland's national independence.

12

I am a devout monarchist and passionate believer in the patriarchy, heredity, and a sensible class system. They are as old as the most ancient societies ever recorded. The Soviet Union, which abolished its ancient traditions in October 1917, descended into an abyss from which it might be argued it has yet properly to emerge. But if there is to be a system of titles and honours then they should be awarded for service over and above the normal call of (paid) duty to one's monarch and country, or to immediate members of the Royal House. Where people have behaved treacherously, their titles should be revoked, as indeed many were from time to time. But not nearly enough.

SC Williamson, writing in 1939, (*The English Tradition in the World*) deplored the lesser role the traditional nobles were playing, even then: "It is a serious thing that England is losing the service of the aristocracy. Throughout history, man has endeavoured to establish and develop, within the whole, 'The Best'".

The second object of this book was to show the involvement in this period, where possible, of the ancient Scottish family of Lauder. Over the centuries they played a prominent, loyal and patriotic role in Scotland's affairs, as will be gleaned from the narrative, and did not need to be bought off by the Crown. As so many of our Scottish histories have been written since the Union of the Crowns many minor barons and lairds of Scotland have found themselves almost extinguished from the annals. Yet without their participation, Scottish history would be entirely different.

By far the greater involvement in all Scotland's affairs was by these barons. They provided the bulk of the forces - feudal levies - every time there was a national conflict. They provided many of the Civil Service and lawyers, and very often, also, sons of the Church. They were generally loved and respected in their respective baronies and lands unless they were outright tyrants. When Parliament assembled the attendance of these magnates would swell the chamber to overflow.

With the gradual abolition of the feudal system as a form of government in Scotland, coupled with Death Duties, the majority of these families appear to have gently faded into unwarranted obscurity. Haddingtonshire or East Lothian, for many centuries the particular stronghold of the Sinclairs, Hays, Lauders, and Hepburns boasts virtually none of them today.

Whilst a handful of power-seekers, including the Stewarts, the Douglases, the Hamiltons and the Homes, to name but a few, spent most of their time and energies conspiring against each other and/or the monarch, and usually involving hundreds, if not thousands of ordinary folk in inter-family battles, many of the nobility sought only what was best for Scotland and its lawful monarch.

The end result of the whole sorry mess that was Scottish politics was that the utterly unscrupulous lost little.

Montecucoli said "In order to wage war a nation must have money, and money, and yet more money". Yet Scotland suffered endless wars and feuds and a particularly violent backlash against the Roman Catholic Church in the Reformation. In the end, the nation was beggared. The Calvinist religious zeal brought Scotland into the Great Civil War against their own, Scottish Stewart monarch, which led directly to his beheading. By the time Cromwell consolidated his hold on Scotland it was politically, morally and financially bankrupt.

The 18th Century Scottish historian Dalrymple noted that at the time of the 1707 Union with England, Scotland was "the poorest kingdom in Europe."

There were those who profited greatly from this period. James VI and Charles I had ennobled many north of the Border in an attempt to curry favour and support. In true form, many betrayed them. After dealing Charles decisive defeats in England, the Scots then shamelessly changed sides and challenged Cromwell in Scotland, supporting Charles II when he landed there. The result was that many of these traitors were further ennobled! Yet those who had remained loyal and had their lands devastated and confiscated by the Commonwealth rarely saw reinstatement after the Restoration, their properties being coveted by lawyers, double-dealers and the unscrupulous.

I come across many people, in North America particularly, who appear to have some hazy glorious vision of Scots fighting (and presumably nearly always winning) great battles against the dreadful English.

It is of course a fantasy. No country with such a tiny population could ever hope to defeat their much larger, richer, neighbour in the long term. Real Scottish history makes sad reading. A hopeless alliance with France caused the Scots far more trouble than it was worth, and yet they honourably adhered rigidly to it.

Scots' tactics and strategies in battles were generally appalling, whether it be, for instance, Haildon Hill, Flodden, or Dunbar. They would have done well to have had a crystal ball and to have been able to read what Carl von Clausewitz wrote in *On War* about Frederick the Great's strategy: "He undertook nothing beyond his powers and *just enough* to gain his object."

Two further quotes from Treitschke place the entire book that you are about to read into context. "It is a function of the State to preserve internal order" (*International Law*), and "The possession of a powerful and well disciplined Army is a sign of great excellence in a nation" (*The Army*). There was little internal order and no proper army. By Treitschke's maxim Scotland was doomed to failure.

Campaigning with the Scots and the Lauders will show to the reader what is meant by the comments I have made in this introduction.

I hope that students of history will find this summary interesting enough for it to be an insight on many details of history sometimes lacking in general text-books.

Lastly I would like to thank Dick New and the staff of Northbrook College in West Sussex for the assistance that they afforded me back in 1993 in the initial preparation of this work, and my friend Stephen Bowyer for his invaluable intial help with the typing, and support.

GREGORY LAUDER-FROST,
Mordington, Berwickshire (Revised in 2016).

*"Our Scottish history is aflame with patriotism.
We will never let that flame recede.
It will ever be a great joy to me that I was
able to give my country a soldier."*

- Sir Harry Lauder (1870-1950),
  15th January, 1915, writing after his only
  son had left for France, never to return.

Chapter 1

1054

By the second half of the eleventh century the King of Scots ruled an area which comprised the old Kingdoms of Pictland, Dalriada and Strathclyde. The most recent accession of territory was the Anglian-inhabited area of the Lothians, until then part of Northumbria where Edinburgh was the most northern part. The Scandanavian Kings retained Orkney, Shetland, the Western Isles, Caithness and some other settlements on the mainland.

There occurred at that time an event which has been made common knowledge by William Shakespeare. In 1040 Duncan I, King of Scots, was murdered by his kinsman, Macbeth, who based his claim to the crown on his wife's royal descent. It is thought by many historians that Duncan wished to alter the ancient Pictish rules of succession, which were matrilineal, to those of primogeniture, to secure the throne for his son, Malcolm, commonly called *Canmore*.

Malcolm fled to London where he languished at the English Court. He was not, however, completely idle, and spent a great deal of his time engaged in trying to curry favour with the Danish father-in-law of the weak English King Edward the Confessor. He was the ruthless Godwin, Earl of the West Saxons, and England was governed, in reality, by him, his equally ruthless sons, and Edward's many Norman advisors and friends. It was Godwin's son, Harold, who usurped the throne upon Edward's death and who, in turn, met his own demise at the battle of Hastings in 1066.

Whilst England was essentially still an Anglo-Saxon kingdom there were already a great number of Norman "immigrants". The Normans were originally Vikings who between 911 and 933 established themselves on the coast of France in territory that came to bear their name: Normandy - land of the Northmen. They spoke Scandinavian, but before long began to adopt French customs and the old French tongue. However in lower Normandy, Scandinavian customs lingered. In 1047 a civil war broke out between those lords in the south who wished to retain the old ways, and Duke William II who was a Francophile. The Duke, with the help of King Henry I of France, crushed the revolt. The next decade, however, saw the Normans turn on and defeat Henry I, their former ally, and also a Papal army which supported him. Some of those knights defeated in 1047 chose to seek their future and fortunes in England. Certainly some had acquired great estates from either the Church or monarch whilst others remained knights, in the true sense of the word, seeking adventure and, where possible, rewards for their service. Today, we would call such people mercenaries.

Edward The Confessor agreed with Malcolm Canmore that the time had come for him to regain his crown from Macbeth and avenge Duncan's murder. In 1054 Malcolm began gathering serious supporters, the most prominent being Siward, Earl of Northumberland, said to be his maternal uncle, or cousin. However we know that Siward was a Dane who probably came to England with Cnut. Before 1041 he was already Earl of the southern (York) Danish part of Northumbria. Upon his marriage he received the northern hereditary Earldom of Northumberland as well. He was then in possession of the whole of Northumbria, from Humber to Tweed. He appears to also have been Earl of Huntingdon from sometime after 1050 when he was addressed as such in a charter dated between 1050 and 1052 and it is thought that the Earldom of Northampton was also bestowed upon him. Under instruction from 'The Confessor' to assist Malcolm, Earl Siward invaded Scotland in 1054 with a large army, many of whom were Norman mercenary knights. One of those was Sir Robertus de Lawedre (sometimes spelt Lavedre as the 'u' was written as a 'v').

Many, if not most, items of the dress and armour worn, and the weapons used by the Norman Knights could be seen in much of north-western Europe at this time, and were not specific to them alone. A glance at the famous Bayeux Tapestry gives us a good idea of the appearance and equipment of the Normans. The mounted Knight's most important weapon was his sword. The type used in the 11th century was a double-edged cutting or slashing sword. It had a blade about 31 inches in length, tapering slightly towards the point. It was razor-sharp, but both hard and flexible. (Axes were not popular with horsemen at this time). The other main weapon of the Knight was his lance, a plain ash shaft fitted with an iron head of leaf or lozenge shape, and with a fairly long socket. The Norman knight was the shock element in the armies of the day, working in groups or 'conrois' comprising perhaps 25 or 50 men. The initial charge with a couched lance was begun at a trot, only breaking into a gallop at the last moment, so as not to tire the horses or lose formation. The lance was held upright at the start and only levelled on nearing the enemy.

The strong contingent of Normans, with their training and experience, gave Malcolm's army a distinct advantage. The campaign began in earnest with Siward invading in 1054 resulting in a major defeat for Macbeth at Dunsinane (where Siward's son, Osbarn, fell in battle) on 27th July. There was then a lull in the fighting while Canmore regrouped. In 1055 Siward died in York. The decisive defeat for Macbeth came with the Battle of Birnham Wood in 1056 at which Robertus de Lawedre signally distinguished himself by his prowess in the field. Macbeth was eventually slain by Malcolm at Lumphanan, on 15th August, 1057.

For these services de Lawedre was rewarded with large grants of land in the Lothians and Berwickshire, and also a portion of Macbeth's lands in Morayshire[1], an estate named Quarrelwood. He fixed his winter seat in the beautiful dale of the Leader Water, naming the district, it is said by Royal Command, after his own surname - Lauderdale. Of these lands he and his heirs were appointed hereditary bailies by King Malcolm III at the Parliament of Forfar, at which time also the newly crowned sovereign changed the Scottish Thanes into Earls, granting them extensive lands and Royal privileges with their titles.

---

[1] Young, 1884; Stewart-Smith, 1898.
Phillimore, R.P.,*North Berwick & District*, North Berwick, 1913, p.47; Ellis, Peter Berresford, p.103 *Macbeth*, London,1980.

Hugo de Morville (died 1162) an Anglo-Norman favourite of King David 1st, *The Saint*, and who became by his hand Constable of Scotland, was later given the Lordship of Regality & feudal superiority of lands in Lauderdale but it did not include everything, terminating a few miles above Earlston and not extending to the Merse. The de Morville Lordship eventually passed to the Douglases. A.Thomson, writing in *Lauder & Lauderdale*, (1902) says of these families, including the Maitlands of Thirlestane, that "the Lauders of that Ilk were the earlier family".

To the barons also, Malcolm gave the right of 'pit and gallows', by which they had the power to erect gibbets for the men and draw-wells wherein to drown the women whom they adjudged worthy of death, upon their own lands. Many of the oldest charters contain the words *cum fossa et furca* – under which pretext, in lawless times, unwarrantable cruelties were perpetrated with impunity.

Just above the Leader Water, the Lauders erected a Norman Keep with flying buttresses[1], a Tower House or Pele. Around this, as was common practice in feudal Europe, a new hamlet grew and although the Tower has now gone, that town, called Lauder after its founder, remains. *The Grange of St Giles* states that the site of Lauder Tower was then (1898) covered by a market garden. Camden (1551 - 1623), in his *Britannia* said that Lauder had 40 houses and cottages. The *Lauderdale Accounts* record that the tower was taken down in 1700.

Lower, in his *Patronymica Britannica,* said that there were no territorial surnames in Scotland before the twelfth century and that they were unusual before the thirteenth. But we know that de Lavedre was, as shown in the *Lamberton Charter,* designated so at the time of his entry into Scotland. Burke positively states that Lauder's name was given to his lands and goes on to say that about 1000 AD Normans had begun assuming family surnames and that this practice

---

[1] *Lauder Tower had stood close by the east side of the present parish church of Lauder. In his famous book* Scottish Rivers *Sir Thomas Dick Lauder states that the tower had "massive walls and towering buttresses".*

gradually extended itself to Britain. A glance at the ancient *Liber Sancte Marie de Melros* shows that the entries made circa 1153 make a clear distinction between the *acqua de Leder* and *terras in territorio de Lauuedir*. James Young, writing in 1884, demolishes any suggestion that the Lauders of that Ilk (meaning 'of those lands') took their name *from* a geographical location.

At the eastern extremity of their great Lowland estates the Lauders built a traditional Norman keep upon The Bass island, commonly called 'Bass Rock', the greater part of which had been granted to them by Canmore. According to *The Bass Rock*, (written by several scholars in 1847), the Lauders are the earliest recorded proprietors of that island. Over the years the fortress was added to, and a substantial castle developed. The northern part of the island had upon it an ancient chapel, a cell beneath it dating from the early ninth century, and this was dedicated to an obscure pious Scottish saint, Baldred. Naturally this meant the church held the superiority of this little part of the island. However, such was the power and influence of the Laird of the Bass that by 1316 we find the Church transferring their part of the Bass to the then feudal baron, Sir Robert de Lawedre, "for his homage and service". Walter MacFarlane gave a very interesting description of the Bass in his *Geographical Collections of Scotland*, published in the first half of the 18th century, He states that it is "on all parts [sides] perpendicular, declining to the south and ascending to the north, in circuit scarce a mile. It has grass for feeding of sheep on all the surface, and well-spring of fresh water near to the top. One of the considerable Barons of the Shire had his residence many times in it". This of course relates to the Lauders.

Lauder of Haltoun (pronounced "Hatton"). Thee Saracen's head commemorates Sir Robert de Lawedre's participation in the Third Crusade under Richard *Coeur-de-Lion*

The Bass is also famous as Europe's greatest nesting and breeding ground for the Solan goose, or gannet, a white sea-fowl. When the family of Lauder of The Bass split into two distinct branches c1390, a younger son at Haltoun (pronounced Hatton) near Ratho, Midlothian, and the other on The Bass, the latter senior branch eventually took as their crest a Solan Goose sitting on a rock. They also adopted the motto "Sub Umbra Alarum Tuarum.", meaning "under the shadow of thy wings". This is taken from Psalm LXIII, verse 8 - "Because thou has been my helper, therefore under the shadow of thy wings will I rejoice".

Lauder of Bass (supporters not shown)

In about the year 1000 the Normans commenced using the kite-shaped shield. In this form, the lower edge of the shield was drawn down to a point, ideal for horsemen. Many of these shields were decorated, especially with wavy crosses and beasts, such as two-legged dragons -

forerunners of Heraldry. The Lauders bore a griffin *rampant* for their armorial figure and this was emblazoned on their shields. The de l'Estoubeillon family of Brittany bears nearly identical arms to those of Lauder of Haltoun, bar the Saracen's head, though no family connection has yet been traced. Alexander Nisbet claimed that anyone bearing a griffin probably had German or Flemish origins, given that up until the middle of the twelfth century almost all those with coats of arms containing a griffin were from families originating in Germany or Flanders. Interestingly, the earliest surviving shield is not Norman, but belonged to the von Brienze family, and dates from the late 1100s.

The Lauder of The Bass coat of arms became surrounded by a Royal *Tressure*, a double orle enriched with fleur-de-lys. Nisbet says that "the double tressure is not allowed to be carried by any subject without a special warrant from the sovereign" and in the case of the Lauders "for those who have merited well of their King and country, as a special additament of honour."

Here then, is an overview of the first Lauders and their seats in the Lowlands, their estates being very substantial. Over the years sons were given parts of these for themselves, in fee or by lease or tack, from the head of the family's 'stock' which in turn relieved the latter of some of his burdens (taxes, raising forces from that particular barony for war etc.). However, as the family grew, so the various branches and relatives became involved in affairs of State, and even more battles.

Chapter 2

HOLY WARS

Any reader of Scottish history will be intrigued, if not stunned, by the almost constant warring right up to the Union of Crowns, and then that of England and Scotland, both within Scotland itself and with others, notably England. The Kingdom of Scots had been forged by successive processes of resistance; resistance to the Romans, to the Picts, to the Anglians, to the Irish, to the Norsemen.

While William the Conqueror was consolidating his conquest of England, Malcolm III and, as already noted, Sir Robert de Lawedre or Lauder, established themselves firmly in Scotland. Malcolm's dynastic marriage to the previously exiled Anglo-Saxon Princess, St.Margaret, also brought with it European innovations to the Scottish Court, as well as introducing other new families to Scotland, notably the Drummonds, who came with Margaret from Hungary. They would remain forever faithful to the Scottish Crown down through the centuries.

Malcolm began to pursue an expansionist policy with the aim of pushing his southern frontier to the river Tees, reviving the old Scottish claim on Northumberland, which, in 1061, Malcolm invaded, wasted the country, and, says Simeon of Durham, "violated the peace of St.Cuthbert" a sacred compact originally made between Malcolm and Tostig Godwinson, sometime Earl of Northumberland, over the relics of the saint in the island of Lindisfarne. In 1070 Malcolm again entered England through Cumberland, laid waste the district of Teesdale and advanced to Cleveland. Finding that Danish and Saxon allies were not there to meet him he retreated through the bishopric of Durham marking his progress with fire and sword, in which neither church nor sanctuary was spared and giving no quarter to either age or sex.

These inroads of Malcolm's were checked by William the Conqueror in 1072, who marched north with a great army and was received, peaceably by Malcolm, at Abernethy. Realising his forces' inferiority he acknowledged William as his overlord and conceded to him Cumberland; this politic submission perhaps prevented William from hammering the Scots as Edward 1st was to do two centuries later. However, this made Cumberland one of the 'debatable' lands which would be cause for future conflict between England and Scotland.

In 1092 the English King William 'Rufus' erected a castle at Carlisle to serve as an additional barrier against Scottish incursions but which Malcolm decided was an infringement of his 'rights' in Cumberland, where he, who still held lands there, was now technically a vassal. In the winter of 1093 Malcolm III again crossed the Border and pillaged the northern parts of Northumberland as far as Alnwick. On St.Brice's Day, 13th November, the Scottish army was encamped on the high ground one mile north of Alnwick Castle.

Robert de Mowbray, Seigneur of Bazoches and Governor of Bamburgh Castle, was then Earl of Northumberland, and the defence of the county depended on him. He was ably assisted by his steward, Morel, who, astonishingly, happened to be Malcolm's godfather.

They were unable to engage in open combat with the vastly superior Scottish army but managed to attack them by surprise and throw them into confusion. Malcolm was slain and Edward, his eldest son, mortally wounded. The story of his death is described in the *Chronicle of Alnwick Abbey.*

> "Malcolm was there mortally wounded near a certain spring, leaving his own name to that spring even for ever. Hence that spring is called in the native English tongue, Malcolmswell. This King Malcolm was wounded by Hamund, then Constable of the said Eustace de Vescy, with a certain lance, on the point of which he had placed

the Keep of the castle of Alnwick for a pledge, as if placing the castle with all its inhabitants in subjection to Malcolm, King of Scotland. This deed being done, Hamund returned with a quick step, sound, unhurt, and whole, passing over a ford of water immensely great, and then by the Divine Will overflowing above measure, and leaving his own name to this ford; whence the ford where he passed over is called, in the native English tongue, Hammund's Ford from that day and thenceforward".

This account must have been written some years later as it appears erroneous. Eustace de Vesci only came into possession of the Barony of Alnwick ninety-two years after Malcolm's death! From an early period a cross stood on the spot where tradition says Malcolm was slain. Half a mile north of Alnwick are the ruins of St.Leonard's Hospital, founded between 1193 and 1216 by Eustace de Vesci for the Soul of Malcolm, King of the Scots. Near the north side of the chapel is Malcolm's well, where the monarch died. A quarter of a mile higher up the hill is Malcolm's Cross, the traditional spot where he received his death wound. Part of the base and upper limit of the cross still survive in the plantation, but a new one was erected in 1774 by Elizabeth, Duchess of Northumberland, a descendant of Malcolm.

Templar grave at Tyninghame

We now move on to Malcolm's son, King David I, *The Saint*, who succeeded to the throne in 1124. He too had spent his youth at the English Court and, impressed by the efficiency of the feudal system imported by the Normans, built upon his mother's modernising efforts and brought it more fully into his own kingdom. Returning from England he brought to Scotland more immigrant landowners and knights who subsequently became feudal barons and superiors. David was principally responsible for the importation of monasticism and all the great offices common to the Courts of Europe, and eventually largely succeeded in bringing to his country the culture and organisation of a European kingdom.

The death of Henry I of England left in 1135 a disputed succession, and David, supporting the claims of his niece, Henry's daughter the Holy Roman Empress Matilda, decided that this was a convenient justification for launching another invasion of northern England.

During the Christmas season of 1136 the Scottish army rapidly occupied Carlisle, Wark, Alnwick, Norham and Newcastle. However, an Anglo-Norman army under another claimant, Stephen of Blois, halted the Scottish advance. Not to be stopped so easily, the Scots invaded again in 1137, negotiated another armistice, and returned again in January 1138. A serious campaign developed in which Stephen's army now ravaged the Lowlands, as an object lesson to the rest of Scotland. Yet his campaign petered out as his army disintegrated through maladministration and betrayal (and, one would think, the severe weather at that time of year). King David again seized the initiative and while an army under his own command was advancing to Newcastle, a column under his nephew William defeated an English blocking force at Clitheroe in Lancashire.

In the summer of 1138 the influential English baron Eustace Fitz-John went over to David, taking with him his castles at Alnwick and Malton. Thus encouraged, the Scots launched yet another and even greater offensive which was now to be met by an army under Archbishop Thurston of York. But the Galloway troops plundered to such an extent that it undermined David's position, as the English (or Anglo-Norman) northern Barons united in a resolve to put an end to these repeated Scottish forays.

On the 22nd August the two forces drew up above North Allerton, Yorkshire, in what was to become known as the Battle of the Standard, owing to the presence on the English side of the holy banners of St Peter of York, St John of Beverley and St Wilfred of Ripon. "Joanni Lawedre, filio secunda de Laudertown," is recorded as being amongst the mounted knights under Prince Henry, King David's son, on the Scottish right.

A serious stalemate developed during the battle and attempting to break it, Prince Henry and his knights crashed straight through the English line and disappeared in the direction of the English tethered horses and North Allerton. The Scots failed to take advantage of the gap made and the English closed ranks. Prince Henry's cavalry found themselves marooned and outnumbered behind enemy lines and ditched their standards and escaped unnoticed, as without identification it was difficult to know just whose knights they were!

The superior numbers of the English and the faulty strategy of the Scots cost the latter the battle and David was forced to retreat. Notwithstanding this defeat, David was able to temporarily advance the frontier of his domain to the rivers Tees and Eden.

About 1170 we find Sir Robert de Lawedre, Knt., a descendant of his namesake, witnessing a charter of John de Mautelant [Maitland] to the Abbey of Dryburgh.[1]

David's grandson, William 'the Lion', who had ascended the Scottish throne in 1165, put his grandfather's new feudal systems further to the test when in 1172 he too invaded England in an unsuccessful attempt to regain the county of Northumberland, which, in the meantime, had once more been lost to the Scots. Sir Robert de Lawedre accompanied William on this campaign - a militarily minor affair but politically of great importance.

Seven years later the eldest son of Henry II plotted with William to overthrow his own father, and it was for this purpose that William again crossed the Border. But the incursion achieved little and a truce was arranged between the two monarchs. But two years later a new invasion was mounted by a large Scottish army, said to number 80,000, including many Flemish mercenaries. The chronicler Fantosme, tells us:

"The town of Belford was first attacked,
Over all the country they scattered themselves;
Some run to towns to commit their folly,
Some go to take sheep in their folds,
Some go to burn towns, I cannot tell you more;
Never will such great destruction be heard spoken of.
Then might you see peasants and Flemings who tie them,
And lead them in their cords like heathen people,
Women fly to the minster, each was ravished,
Naked without clothes, she forgets there her property;

---

[1] Young, 1884, and Stewart-Smith, 1898.

A, God! why did William de Vesci not know it?
The booty were rescued, not would they have failed in it.
They burnt the country; but God was a friend
To those gentle peasants who were defenceless,
For the Scots were not their mortal enemies;
They would have beaten, slain and ill-treated them all."

Although Northumberland was laid waste, William achieved little. Failing to take Prudhoe Castle he moved north to besiege Alnwick. At this stage he had with him only 500 knights, while the mass of his army pillaged the country around. They burnt the town of Warkworth and slew 300 men, women and children, who had taken refuge in the church of St.Lawrence.

Meanwhile, a small number of knights led by Odinel de Umfraville, Lord of Prudhoe, had advanced quickly from Newcastle to assist the defenders of Alnwick Castle. A spy they had sent in advance reported to them that William 'the Lion' was encamped in a field a quarter of a mile west of the castle with only sixty knights awaiting the arrival of their main forces, and meantime had settled down to a meal. The English troops decided to attack:

"The King of Scotland was brave, wonderful, and old,
Before Alnwick he stood unarmed.
When these had once cried the war signal of Vesci,
And 'Glanville knights!' and 'Baliol!' likewise,
Odonel de Umfraville raised a cry of his own,
And this of Estuteville, a bold knight;
The knew William that he was nearly betrayed,
Quickly he stirred himself, he was not disconcerted."

A brief struggle ensued and William and most of his attendants were taken prisoner, Sir Robert de Lawedre, however, escaped under cover of darkness back to Scotland. A monument in the Gothic style stands in Rotton Row, Alnwick, commemorating the siege and the King's capture. William was subsequently released and in 1186 married

Ermengarde, whose grandmother was an illegitimate daughter of the English King Henry I.

In 1188 Sir Robert de Lawedre reappears on the scene as one of the Scottish nobles who accompanied William 'the Lion's brother, David, Earl of Huntingdon, to fight in the Third Crusade - a Holy War - under the banner of the Cross and beneath the standard of Richard I of England, *Coeur-de-Lion.*[2] As an emblem of his presence in Palestine, Sir Robert added a severed Saracen's head on a sword to his arms.[3]

It was also William 'the Lion' who erected the town-lands of Lauder into a Royal Burgh, thus giving his brother's companion-in-arms' town many special privileges. David, Earl of Huntingdon, married, before his departure for Palestine, Matilda d'Avranches, daughter of Hugh de Kevelioc (1147-1181), 6th Earl of Chester, a well-connected family.

The object of this third Crusade was to rescue the sacred sepulchre at Jerusalem from the hands of Saladin, Sultan of Egypt. All Europe was in arms against the Saracens, kings and emperors fighting alongside Frederick I of Germany, Richard *Coeur-de-Lion* and Philip Augustus of France. Fired with enthusiasm, thousands braved death and danger most triumphantly for the glory of The Church and the honour of knighthood. Regretfully most found only a grave beneath the burning sun of Palestine. A few hundreds did return to their families and their homes, and among that few was our brave crusader Robert de Lawedre, who was then styled *fifth Baron.*

King William 'The Lion' died at Stirling on 4th December 1214 aged 72 and the next serious conflict to affect Scotland and which is well documented, was the succession crisis following the death of his grandson, Alexander III in 1286. He left no heirs-male and amongst the claimants the two main ones were the Anglo-Normans John de

[2] Holinshed, pps.277-278.
[3] "Lauder Arms" in *The Double Tressure,* No.29, 2007, Heraldry Society of Scotland, pps:20-39.

Balliol, Lord of Barnard Castle, and Robert de Brus (1210-1295), Lord of Annandale and grandfather of "The Bruce". Both were descendants of David I, in the female line, Balliol the senior.

John Balliol was subsequently awarded the Crown and crowned King of Scots on St.Andrew's Day 1292 following arbitration at the castle of Berwick-upon-Tweed by King Edward I of England, an unenviable beginning for anyone. Relations between England and Scotland began almost immediately to deteriorate. In 1295 Balliol and the Scots formed with France what was to become known as the *Auld Alliance,* something that became an enduring affinity between the two countries.

The following year Edward I, with a great army (Miller states it was only 12000 men) under John de Warrene, 7th Earl of Surrey (and father of John de Balliol's wife) sacked Berwick-upon-Tweed with much bloodshed, and defeated Balliol in a battle near Dunbar. Balliol abdicated on the 10th July 1296, and was taken into captivity to the Tower of London. He was later sent into exile in France where he died at Bailleul in October 1314[1] .

In 1297 Edward 1st of England was occupied with an inconclusive campaign against King Philip IV of France. The Scots' nationhood was possibly forged at this time as they swung into rebellion against the feudal overlordship of Edward behind their great hero, Sir William Wallace. Professor Barrow suggests that he was a descendant of Richard Wallace, holder of a garrison-serjeant's fee in Shropshire under William FitzAlan in 1166. Richard appears to have been endowed by William's brother, Walter FitzAlan 'the Steward', with the lands south of Kilmarnock on which he founded Riccarton – Richard's town. Barrow states that "it is all but certain that Wallace belonged to the family brought to Scotland from Shropshire in the train of Walter FitzAlan." One of the foremost supporters of Wallace

---

[1] Half of the fulling-mill and half of the Mains of Lauder had been in Sir John de Balliol's possession, and these now passed to the Lauders who already owned the other halves. A confirmation of this appears in Great Seal Charters granted to Alan Lauder of that Ilk & Whitslaid in 1371.

was yet another Sir Robert de Lawedre, designated "great Laird of Congalton and The Bass" (Congalton is west of North Berwick).

Berwick Marygate

Sir Robert is described as Wallace's "trusty friend and faithful companion in arms from the beginning of his career to the sad ending of his heroic life. Sir Robert defended his fortress-island of The Bass with great determination against Edward 1st, and in his staunch loyalty to his country none could seduce him from his allegiance. Such was his eagerness to march with Wallace against Patrick 7th Earl of Dunbar, who had espoused the English cause, that he would rather have lost his beloved Bass than have been denied this gratification."[4] This feud with the pro-English Earl makes interesting reading.[5]

---

[4] Stewart-Smith, 1898.
[5] The Earl of Dunbar, with the Earl of Angus, Robert de Brus the elder, and his son Robert de Brus, Earl of Carrick (later King), swore fealty to the English king at Wark, Northumberland, on 25th March 1296.

Wallace, with 200 men, went in pursuit of Dunbar and was joined by Sir Robert de Laweder at Musselburgh, and afterwards by Crystal Seton. They were met at Linton by 'Squire Lyle' [probably Lyle of Stoneypath near Garvald in East Lothian], who informed them that the Earl had gathered a force of 900 men at Cockburnspath and was marching towards Dunbar. Sir Robert de Lawedre "was in a hurry to get thither" but Wallace did not rush his men. The two sides met in a field near Innerwick and "after a terrible conflict" the Earl of Dunbar was compelled to retreat to Cockburnspath while Wallace fell back on Dunbar where he placed the Earl's vacated castle in the charge of Crystal Seton. He then went in pursuit of the fugitive Earl. But the Earl of Dunbar had gone on to Northumberland and returned with vessels to blockade Dunbar and 20,000 men in order to retake his castle.

Wallace returned to the fray and was joined by the Hays, the Ramsays and the Grahams, and his chosen cavalry. With 5000 men they marched to attempt the relief of the besieged Seton. They were, however, ambushed at nearby Spott by the Bishop of Durham who had come to the assistance of the Earl of Dunbar, and Wallace found himself hemmed in. Fortunately scouts from Dunbar castle had advised Seton of the situation and he rode out to relieve Wallace. We are told that "the two armies closed in mortal strife."

William Wallace

The desperate valour of Wallace and his supporters appeared to little avail. The Earl of Dunbar wounded Wallace who is said to have returned the blow "sevenfold", hurting Mautelant [Maitland] who had

38

thrown himself between the two adversaries! Wallace's horse was killed beneath him but "500 resolute warriors rescued their champion, and the war-torn armies were glad to retire." The Earl, Bishop Beik, and Robert de Brus retired to Norham, Northumberland, and a short peace was concluded.[6]

Among Blind Harry's other ballads about Wallace is to be found the following passage, in which he tells about other help Wallace and his fighters got from Sir Robert de Laweder of The Bass:

Cetoun [Seton], Lauder and Richard off Lunde,
In a gud barge thai past about be se;
Sanct Jhonstoun hawyn thair ankyr haiff thai set
Twa Inglis schippis thai tuk with outyn let
The tane thai brunt, syn stuffyt the tothir weill
With artailze, and stalwart men in steyll,
To kep the port, that suld com na wictaill
In to that toun, nor men at mycht them waill.

If translation is needed, this poem tells how Lauder and his friends set out by boat from the Forth, going north round Fife Ness and into the Tay estuary, then up-river to the harbour at Perth, where they easily captured two English ships, burning one and using the other as a fortified block-ship so that the English garrison at Perth was blockaded by river.

We find Lauder again present with his hero at the famous battle of Stirling Bridge, which occurred on the 12th September 1297 where Wallace gained a most complete victory over Edward's Governor of Scotland, the ageing John de Warenne, 7th Earl of Surrey. The ill-fated and much detested Sir Hugh Cressingham was slain with thousands of his followers when, at the outset, he led the van of the doomed Englishmen who attempted to cross the bridge. It would have been better for them if they had listened to the advice of the Scottish traitor, Sir Richard Lundie, (who by this time had changed sides) and

---

[6] Miller, 1830.

never set foot upon that long, narrow wooden way, which led them like sheep to slaughter and a watery grave.

Norham Castle, on the Tweed, in 1728

Wallace, on foot, "with a grate scharp spere" was in the thickest of the fight and with his own hand slew Cressingham, the English King's Treasurer. Ten thousand were said to have been killed, and another seven thousand drowned without mercy, leaving but a poor straggling remnant of the invading army, who set fire to the bridge in order to prevent the Scots from pursuing them. This old wooden bridge stood about a mile above the spot where the present stone one was erected shortly afterwards. Following the battle, the Earl of Surrey retreated to the vicinity of Berwick-upon-Tweed to await his King.

Daring exploits and marvellous successes followed this unexpected victory and we find Sir Robert de Lawedre often mentioned as being among those Scottish knights who, in the hour of their country's need, rose grandly to any occasion. In the summer of 1298, Edward assembled a force of 15000 men, including 2500 cavalry, at York. Marching into Scotland his army's morale was constantly sapped by the hide-and-seek exercises in which Wallace engaged. However, on the 22nd July the English army encountered Wallace near Falkirk, the latter's force being numerically inferior.

Taking part was not only Sir Robert de Lawedre of The Bass but also his eldest son, Robert, *fils* (junior). Wallace employed very clever defensive tactics placing himself between Callender Wood, the Westquarter Burn, and marshland. But confusion was at hand. The English knights charged and as they did the Scottish cavalry suddenly retired from the field leaving their archers to be summarily ridden down. The Scottish spearmen melted away under a hail of English arrows and the English cavalry charged in amongst them inflicting considerable slaughter. Wallace escaped through the forest.

Seven years later Sir William Wallace was betrayed, it is said, by Sir John Monteith, whom he thought his friend. Wallace was captured, his hands bound, and taken to England where, on the 23rd August 1305, Scotland's grandest warrior was executed – hanged, drawn and quartered. The nation now had a martyr.

Sir Robert de Lawedre of The Bass, senior, was devastated by the loss of his friend and hero Wallace and although he continued in his support of Scotland's sovereignty he was by now quite old and exhausted and in 1311 he died. A stone, with the relief of a knight lying on his back with his hands clasped around a great sword upon his breast was placed over his last resting place in the Auld Kirk on the shore at North Berwick, Upon the stone was engraved *here lies the good Robert Lauder, the great Laird of Congalton and the Bass, who died May, 1311*. Interestingly, according to Nisbet, who examined the gravestone in 1718, the inscription was cut in Saxon letters, evidence of the Anglian influence in the Lowlands. Large sections of this tombstone are now in the care of the East Lothian County Council, after having been buried and assumed lost for over one hundred years.

Robert 'The Bruce' was of Anglo-Norman stock, like many of his class. His father, whilst being Robert de Brus of Annandale, and Earl of Carrick in right of his wife, was never-the-less an English Peer, Baron de Brus (cr.1295) who fought with King Edward 1st in the battle of Dunbar in 1296 and, when approaching death in 1304, requested that his body be interred not in Scotland but in the Abbey of Holm Cultram, Cumberland. It was his father, another Robert (d.1295 and buried in the family tomb in Guisborough Priory, Cleveland, England), who had been one of the *Competitors* for the Crown of Scotland in right of his mother, a daughter of David 9th Earl of Huntingdon.

Like his forbears, Robert 'The Bruce' also held lands in England (he was born at Whittle, in Essex[7]) and experienced the unavoidable conflict of loyalties. We have already witnessed this above, where at one point The Bruce was a supporter of the Earl of Dunbar who, in turn, was financed by England. Bruce's family were also opposed to John de Balliol (the senior claimant to the throne) and more than once Robert 'The Bruce' made submissions to Edward 1st. Upon the death of his father he may be held to have become Lord Bruce, in the Peerage of England, and he had livery of his father's English lands on 14th June 1304 having done homage to King Edward.

However, in a murderous quarrel between The Bruce and John 'the Red' Comyn, feudal baron of Badenoch, and nephew and supporter of Balliol, Comyn was slain. As he had given his allegiance to Edward, the latter declared The Bruce to be his enemy, giving Robert the chance of asserting his claim to the crown of Scots, in which he was eventually successful. As a result his estates in England were taken into King Edward's hands on 20th February 1305/6, and The Bruce was crowned on 27th March 1306. He spent years in guerrilla warfare winning back his kingdom piecemeal from English garrisons.

---

[7] Thompson, E.M., editor, *The Chronicle of Geoffrey le Baker of Swinbrook*, 1889, p.38.

Chapter 3

A DARK CENTURY

The 14th. Century began badly for Scotland. Sir William Wallace had been executed in London in 1305 and although Robert 'The Bruce' was now on the throne, there was further trouble in store. As we have seen, Wallace's companion, Sir Robert de Lawedre of The Bass, had died in 1311, leaving his son and grandson to carry the colours for their noble family. Sir Andrew Lauder, Bt., writing in the eighteenth century, claimed that over thirty-three of the Lauders of Lauder and The Bass were named Robert, making it sometimes difficult to be accurate.

In 1314, King Edward II of England decided to give his full attention to Scotland and proceeded north with an army of 20,000 men. Stirling castle, the last stronghold of the English in Scotland, was threatened by an army under The Bruce which had massed between the Bannock Burn (white shining stream) and the castle, three miles to the north. They consisted almost entirely of pikemen and were outnumbered by at least three to one by the English foot soldiers and cavalry.

Upon arrival the English Army found themselves confined to a small marsh-bordered area between the Bannock Burn and the river Forth, and so had insufficient room for their cavalry and men to manoeuvre efficiently. By masterly use of the terrain, the Scots overcame the superior numbers of the enemy. Taking advantage of the English forces' confusion, 'The Bruce' attacked. Amongst his knights was almost certainly, as an adherent of 'The Bruce' and a friend and relation of the Earls of Moray and Dunbar (for the latter he witnessed charters)[8], Sir Robert de Lawedre of The Bass (d. Sept 1337) would have taken part in the Battle of Bannockburn 24th June 1314.

The English position soon became hopeless and was settled by a charge down Gillies Hill of some 2000 Scots. The subsequent

---

[8] Young, 1884, p.19.

slaughter was immense and many of those who survived the wrath of the Scots perished in the Bannock Burn and the morasses beyond.

Bannockburn

This was a decisive battle in Scottish history at which the English Crown's overlordship of Scotland was overthrown, with Scotland regaining its independence and which established 'The Bruce' firmly on his throne. In 1320 the nobility of Scotland sent a letter to Pope John XXII, on behalf of the Community of the Realm, announcing their King's achievement and stressing the reality of the situation and asking, in this famous *Declaration of Arbroath,* for His Holiness' recognition of Robert the Bruce as king, and for Scotland as a sovereign nation in its own right.

Sir Robert de Lawedre of The Bass received the Church's portion of that island in 1316 "five years after the good Lairds death" and that in the charter it is noted that this new laird's eldest son, Robert, was also present, as "a page". We also know from ancient charters that Robert 'The Bruce', about 1317, made Sir Robert de Lawedre of The Bass Justiciary of the Lothians, a position, Sir George Mackenzie the great antiquary tells us, was only held by noblemen. Doubtless this appointment was for Sir Robert's loyalty.

"Sir Robert de Lawedre de Bass" also acted on several occasions as an ambassador for Robert 'The Bruce', being one of the signatories to the truce arbitrated by Sire de Sully, a French envoy, and signed at Newcastle-upon-Tyne on the 3rd May 1323, between England and Scotland.[9] England was forced to recognise the reality of the situation the year following the murder of King Edward II. On 7th June 1323 Sir Robert de Lawedre, Knt., took part in a King's Council held by Robert 'The Bruce' at Berwick-upon-Tweed.[10]

King Robert The Bruce, now ageing and diseased and satiated with war, assembled his Peers and barons and proposed a final treaty of peace with the young King Edward III. Again we find Sir Robert de Lawedre the King's chosen ambassador for the ratification of the treaty concluded at Edinburgh on the 17th March 1327/8.[11] Hugh, Earl of Ross and Sir Robert de Lawedre, Justiciary of the Lothians, by special command were also present at Northampton on the 4th May 1328 and acted as proxies for King Robert, swearing the final conditional clause "on the soul of The Bruce".[12]

---

[9] Rymer's *Foedera* vol.iii.p.1022.
[10] *The Acts of the Parliaments of Scotland*, vol.1, 1124-1423, London, 1844, p.110.
[11] Robertson's *Index,* p.101.
[12] Stones, Professor E.L.G., editor, *Anglo-Scottish Relations 1174-1328*, Oxford, 1970, pps:341-5.

Robert The Bruce died at Cardross on the 7th June 1329, and the throne went to his son by his second marriage, David II, aged 5. Sir Robert de Lawedre of The Bass, and his son Robert, showed themselves to be men of sterling merit, with considerable authority in the lands over which they held almost unlimited jurisdiction by virtue of their feudal baronial rights and their high offices in the State during the King's minority. In *The Douglas Book* by Sir William Fraser, KCB LLD., there is a copy of a charter granted by Randolph, Earl of Moray, to John, Earl of Angus, dated 1331, to which the witness is *Roberto de Lawedre, militibus, Justiciario Lowdonie.* "Lord Robert de Lawedre, Justiciar of Lothian and Sheriff of Berwick" witnessed an Indenture on 11th May 1332[13], and at an inquest held at Aberdeen on the 11th September, 1333, he is styled "Sir Robert de Lawedre, Chamberlain of Scotland".[14] [15] [16]

Edward, son of the deposed and exiled King John de Balliol, seeking to overthrow the Bruce dynasty, and assisted by a party of malcontent nobles, surprised and defeated King David Bruce's force at Dupplin on the 22nd September 1332. Balliol thereafter took possession of Perth and was crowned at Scone on the 24th September 1332, acknowledging again King Edward III as his feudal overlord thus surrendering to him the hard-won liberty of the kingdom.

However, his reign was shortlived and on the 16th December Balliol was suddenly attacked at Annan by the Earl of Moray and an assemblage of other barons & knights, defeated, and driven out of Scotland. On the way, at Jedburgh, Balliol's party was waylaid and attacked by an ambush under the command of Archibald Douglas,

---

[13] University of Durham, *Miscellaneous Charters*, no.1169.

[14] Fraser, Sir William, C.B., LL.D., *The Douglas Book*, vol.2, p.587, Edinburgh 1885.

[15] Burnett, George, Lyon King of Arms, editor, *The Exchequer Rolls of Scotland* vol.II, 1359-1379, Edinburgh, 1878, p.cxxiii, 'Chamberlains of Scotland'.

[16] Mackenzie, Sir George, *Precedency*, p.40, "the Chamberlain of Scotland was the third great officer of state".

which, however, was discovered and routed, and Balliol managed to reach Kelso in safety. In this skirmish Robert de Lauder *the younger* was taken prisoner, with others. There must have been an exchange of prisoners shortly after, for we soon hear of him again fighting under the Douglas banner, after Balliol's undignified ride to Carlisle.

The Scottish leaders, having heard from their spies of Balliol's imprudent march from the fortress of Roxburgh to the comparatively defenceless town of Annan, they resolved on a surprise, which was boldly conceived and promptly executed. Marching overnight, the Scots arrived at Annan in the early morning, and finding the hapless Balliol and his followers in their beds, slew about one hundred of them. Balliol himself again escaped, but in such haste that with one limb clothed and another naked he threw himself on a bare-backed steed, and thus fled to Carlisle. His brother, Sir Henry Balliol, who slew many of the attacking party with a stout staff, was at last, with several other knights, overpowered and slain.

This served Edward III as a pretext to aver that the Scots had broken the treaty of Northampton. Edward accordingly threw off his mask, openly espoused the cause of Balliol and with him invaded Scotland, laying siege to the castle of Berwick-upon-Tweed on the 12th April 1333.

The Scots had prepared for this by provisioning the town and putting in a garrison of seasoned troops. Realising the siege would last a long time Edward led the bulk of his army into Scotland, laying waste the country and capturing Edinburgh. Returning to Berwick, Edward established a complete blockade by sea and land, and the inhabitants suffered greatly.

In the meantime, the Scottish Regent, Sir Archibald Douglas, had raised a mighty army to relieve Berwick. In order to draw off Edward's army he marched south and laid siege to Bamburgh Castle where the English Queen was resident. But Edward did not take the bait nor raise the siege of Berwick as he knew that Bamburgh was impregnable.

Berwick-upon-Tweed Castle

With Sir Archibald Douglas was Sir Robert de Lawedre, jnr., usually
designated "of Quarrelwood" (Malcolm Canmore had given the first
Sir Robert this estate in Morayshire also),[17] and Captain of Urquhart
Castle. Realising that their attempt to draw Edward away from
Berwick had failed the Scots returned north and on the 18th July 1333,
crossed the Tweed and encamped at Dunsepark.

As the Scottish army had gone south and the siege became more
desperate, the garrison at Berwick agreed, on the 15th July, to
surrender in five days time if not relieved. The Deputy Governor of
the town, one of Sir Alexander Seton's sons, was handed over as a
hostage to guarantee good faith. Edward had already taken the
younger son prisoner. Now that the Scottish army had crossed the
Tweed, Edward was afraid that the town might be relieved before the
surrender date of the 20th, so he sent an ultimatum that the town must
surrender immediately otherwise he would execute Seton's two sons in

---

[17] In 1328 he had been appointed Justiciary of 'that part of Scotland on the
North side of the Water of Forth' due to his Moray estates.

front of the ramparts. The garrison refused and the two lads, Richard and William, were led out and hanged in sight of their grief-stricken parents who watched from the town walls.

Part of the ruins of Urquhart Castle. Sir Robert Lauder of Quarrelwood was Constable of this castle for several years.

Near the Royal Border Bridge is a small hill called *Hang-a-Dyke Neuk* where the execution is said to have taken place. "Moreover the remains of two human skulls are to be seen at this day in the poor-house of Tweedmouth, which the oldest and most respectable inhabitants of that village affirm to have been handed down from generation to generation as being the skulls of Sir Alexander Seton's two sons".[18]

Douglas now decided to engage in battle with Edward's forces. A marsh divided Halidon Hill outside Berwick from the opposite eminence upon which the Scottish commanders had arranged their forces. Time forced the Scots to fight a pitched battle under

---

[18] Fuller, G. 1799.

unfavourable circumstances. The nature of the ground rendered it impossible for the English position to be attacked by cavalry and many of the Scottish knights dismounted to join the main army which accordingly advanced on foot.

Contrary to the advice of the senior officers, the Scots advanced through the marsh. Edward's three dismounted divisions were each protected with wings of archers. The Scots had badly exposed themselves as defenceless targets to the irresistible volleys of the famous English archers, who riddled them. Thousands were slain. An ancient manuscript tells us "the arrows flew thick as motes in a sunbeam, which no mail-coat could brook".

Extricated at length from the marsh, the Scots attacked the enemy with great fury; but notwithstanding their courage and impetuosity, they were too fatigued to sustain the minor success which had attended their first attack. Those who reached the English lines were soon overcome. Many of the principal Scottish nobles and barons of high rank were slain, and with them fell no fewer than fourteen thousand men. This dreadful defeat took place on the 19th July, and with no hope left the Castle at Berwick surrendered the following day.

Knighton tells us that Sir Robert de Lawedre, senior, was present at the battle "but was too far advanced in age to be able to dismount with his armour on, and therefore he took no active part in the fight", retiring when it became clear that the battle was lost.

Halidon Hill memorial

Sir Archibald Douglas, alongside whom had fought Sir Robert de Lawedre junior, in the third division, fell on the field. His older brother, Sir James Douglas, had gone in 1330, with a band of Scotland's noblest warriors, to carry the heart of The Bruce to the Holy Land (although they had to turn back after being almost decimated by Moors in Spain).

Immediately after the defeat at Halidon Hill, Sir Robert de Lawedre junior, who survived the slaughter, hastened to the north accompanied by Chisholm of that Ilk, who held lands at Paxton, Berwickshire, to occupy and garrison Urquhart Castle on Loch Ness, which, by his brave defence completely defied the power of Edward III, and stands recorded in the nation's annals, associated with the name of Lauder, as one of the five strongholds of Scotland which the English could not take.

Sir Robert de Lawedre of The Bass, senior, was still alive in 1335 when it is recorded that he sent, as his proxy, his brave son, the Captain of Urquhart Castle, as one of the three Scottish Commissioners to deliberate the latest English-Scots peace treaty (the other two commissioners being Andrew Moray and William Douglas).

The old man had had his office of Justiciary reconfirmed only the previous year by Edward III himself, in his regulating of the government after his victory over the Scottish nation. The English monarch deemed it expedient for Sir Robert to continue in the post, it being doubtful that an Englishman could have been found and, also, because Lauder had been originally appointed by The Bruce for the judicial administration of the established laws of the country. On 1337 "Robertum de Lawedre, Justiciarium Laudonie", was a member of the Council of the Regency, and in the printed Exchequer Rolls[19] there is an entry showing a sum of 18 shillings was paid for bringing a boat hired by Sir Robert de Lauder, Justiciarius Laudonie, from The Bass to Aberdeen. He died, however, before December 1337 when his wife was receiving his pension.

The Lauders, however, played a double game. They would continue their support for Scotland. In January 1338 the Earls of Salisbury and Arundel were besieging Dunbar Castle, which was defended by the Countess of Dunbar & March, popularly known as 'Black Agnes' due to a swarthy complexion. The Countess's position was becoming desperate and Sir Alexander Ramsay of the Foulden & Dalhousie family, with forty men, sailed under cover of darkness from The Bass, passed the English ships outside Dunbar – and smuggled supplies to the Countess. In the morning the Countess was able to offer her

---

[19] Vol.1, p.452-3.

enemy food and wine. They, thinking her well supplied, raised the siege and departed. The Lauder castle on The Bass was, at that time, described as "a fortress, a stone castle with a curtain wall over the landing stage."

Moray

Balliol had ceded most of Scotland south of the Forth to Edward III, thereby ensuring a further century of warfare as the Scots fought to recover their lands. By 1341 Perth, garrisoned by Balliol, and

Edinburgh, had been recaptured. Balliol retreated to northern England and David II returned to Scotland from France, whence he had fled.

In the same year the French King, Philip VI, appealed to David to launch a diversion to distract the English who were then laying siege to Calais. In October the Scottish King led an invading army into England, laying waste the countryside and sacking the Abbey of Lanercost in Cumberland as he marched. By the 16th October David had reached Durham and his army camped in the Bearpark. However, the Archbishop of York and the northern English Lords had summoned their forces to assembly at Bishop Auckland. The English Army, numbering approximately 15,000, then deployed on a north-south ridge within sight of Bearpark, near Nevilles Cross, one of several ancient crosses which ringed the City of Durham, and appropriately, Ralph Neville commanded their army.

The Scots, with perhaps 20,000 troops, marched out to meet them. As at Halidon Hill, the English were on a hill some 200 feet above the Scots and the ground seemed little suited to cavalry, the English horse being initially sent to the rear. King David and the erstwhile Sir William Douglas, with Robert the Stewart, and the three divisions under them were, because of the valley and a forward ravine, to present a continuous front. Confusion spread as the Scottish right and centre came together in order to avoid the ravine. This presented an ideal target for the English archers who immediately began to thin them out. On the left, Robert's troops met with greater success and the English line was thrown into some disorder as the Scottish spearmen charged home. The situation was restored when the English brought up their cavalry. Although the Scots put up a fierce fight the battle was lost for them. King David, wounded and exhausted, escaped from the field but was captured during the pursuit. Taken to the Tower of London, he was not to regain his freedom until 1357. We know that Sir Robert de Lawedre was also captured at this battle.[20]

---

[20] *Rotuli Scotiae in Turra Londinensi et in Domo Capitulari Westmonasteriensi asservati*, London, 1814-19, 2 vols. folio.

Sir Robert had succeeded his aged father in late 1337 and he, like his father when he inherited the family lands, was quite old. "Sir Robert de Lawedre, Justiciar of Scotland on the north side of the water of Forth" was present at the siege of Falkland Castle in February 1337.[21] We later find him mentioned in his own right founding a chaplaincy in the Cathedral Church of Moray, which was confirmed by a Royal Writ from King David Bruce at Elgin on the 10th May 1367.

His second son, and eventual heir, was Alan de Lawedre of that Ilk[22], the proprietor of the lands of Whitslade (the ruin of this tower-house is still be seen), Birkenside, Ledgerwood, Monston, Mertoun all in Berwickshire, The Bass, Tynninghame, and the East Lothian estates, Urmonston, Norton, etc., near Ratho, and a whole range of other lands which had been granted to him by the King. Professor Barrow notes that Birkenside & Legerwood were originally and hereditarily in the possession of Walter FitzAlan, 1st High Steward of Scotland who, in 1164, presented the church there to Paisley Abbey.

In 1370 when Alan's father sold part of his land "in and near his burgh of Lauder" to Thomas de Borthwick, a relative, the three witnesses are John Maitland and his brother William (of the family who lived at Thirlestane Tower, three miles south-east of Lauder) and *Roberto filio Alani tunc Ballio de Lawedre* [Robert, son of Alan, Baillie of Lauder]. Alan was married to Alicia, daughter of Sir Colin Campbell of Lochow (d. c1343), progenitor of the Earls & Dukes of Argyll.

This Alan de Lawedre was said by Abercrombie to be "one of the bravest knights that ever drew sword; famous in all martial exercises, renowned in feats of chivalry, and foremost in his country's service." He was also a close confederate of the Earl of Douglas, and Constable and Keeper of Tantallon Castle, one of the Douglas strongholds. Trained under the banner of the good Lord James, he won his spurs

[21] Fraser, Sir William, *The Douglas Book,* vol. 3, Edinburgh, 1885, p.391-2.
[22] Amongst the manuscripts of the Duke of Hamilton, there is a document written by William 1st Earl of Douglas (c1327-1384), who describes Alan Lauder as the second son of Sir Robert Lauder of Quarrelwood and Bass. HMSS Commission, London, 1887, number 126, p.205.

most nobly. (Few leaders could boast, as Douglas did, that he had fought seventy battles, out of which fifty-seven were victorious, and not a scar had marked his face). King Robert II held Alan in such high esteem that he bestowed upon him *una protectione perpetua.*[23] At Scone, on the 11th June 1374, the King conferred upon Alan the lands and barony of Halton [pronounced Hatton] near Ratho, with a further confirmation of same on 26th July 1377.

In 1369 a fourteen year truce with England had been concluded. King Robert II (a Stewart) endeavoured to strengthen Scotland's position by renewing the *Auld Alliance* in 1371. France was once again on the offensive against England and in 1385 a force of one thousand French knights, commanded by the Admiral of France, Jean de Vienne, was sent to Scotland. The arrival of de Vienne's force provoked an English invasion led by King Richard II. The second Earl of Douglas restrained de Vienne from offering battle, while the English King burnt the Abbeys of Melrose, Dryburgh, Newbattle and Holyrood, and devastated Edinburgh. The Scots watched him retire, and then cleared out the English occupying forces, in particular those which had held Teviotdale since the days of Edward Balliol. The French were eager for a full-scale invasion of England and were disgusted to discover that their ally expected them to participate in the usual guerrilla warfare.

Border warfare was endemic throughout most of the 14th century. Major expeditions involving armies of several thousand men were periodically mounted by the Scots to harass the English. In the summer of 1388 James, 2nd Earl of Douglas, led a raid into north-eastern England while Sir Archibald Douglas marched westward by Carlisle with a much stronger column. James plundered county Durham and in a skirmish at the gates of Newcastle, Douglas captured Henry *Hotspur* Percy's lance pennon. (Henry was the son of the Duke of Northumberland, the new but temporary English Keeper of Berwick Castle). The Percys raised an army of 8000 men to redeem

---

[23] *The Great Seal* no.425, 10th March 1372.

their lost honour and set out after the retiring Scots twenty-four hours later.

Douglas became reckless, and against the advice of his commanders, who urged that the army should continue its retreat into Scotland, made camp at Otterburn to give *Hotspur* an opportunity to retake his pennon in battle. As the Scottish camp prepared for the night on the 19th August 1388, the English appeared to the east and *Hotspur*, pausing only to despatch Sir Thomas Umfraville of Harbottle, aged just 25, with 3000 men on an outflanking march to the north, launched an immediate attack in what became in English folklore the Battle of Chevy Chase, a reference to the various forces chasing each other around the Cheviot Hills. The Earl of Douglas commanded 6000 - 7000 men. Forming them in two divisions, he appears to have sent one division forward to hold Percy, while he led the other against the enemy's right flank.

It was by now quite dark and while the English were involved in a melee with the foremost Scottish division, Douglas and his troops crashed into their right. In close quarter combat at night the English longbows were useless and gradually the Scots began to gain the advantage. At some point in the fighting Douglas was killed.

Froissart mentions Sir Robert Lauder (eldest son & heir of Alan) "a renowned hero" having been present at the battle.[24] The English continued to give ground and both *Hotspur* and his brother were captured. Although Umfraville had meanwhile found the Scottish camp and raided it, he nevertheless retreated by the route he had come. The Scots had, by morning, become masters of the field and resumed their march northwards. Graphic pictures of this battle were painted by J. Graham and later engraved in 1822 by P. Dawe.

---

[24] Young, 1884. p.45.

The Norman keep of the castle at Newcastle-upon-Tyne

The conflict was followed by a series of inroads by the border Barons, which continued, without intermission, for over ten years, when a truce was agreed upon between the English and the Scots. This truce was, however, of short duration. Tytler states that the eastern marches were exposed to constant ravages by the Earl of Dunbar and the Percies, the former of whom could not bear to see his vast possessions in the hands of the Douglas. In order to put a stop to these destructive invasions, the Scottish border Barons - "the Hamiltons, the Hepburns, Cockburns and Lauders" – assembled their united power and frequently engaged the common enemy.

One of these occasions occurred in the year 1402 when a little army, under Sir Patrick Hepburn, younger of Hailes, invaded the north of England and laid waste the country "acquiring great booty". Having, however, proceeded too far, Percy and the Earl of Dunbar or March, with a body of Northumbrians, were able to intercept the Scots at Nesbit Moor, on the 22nd June, where a desperate conflict took place.

The Scots were only four hundred strong, and the battle, which had been long, bloody and doubtful, was at last decided by the arrival of George de Dunbar, the Earl's son, with two hundred men – including thirty horse - from the garrison of occupied Berwick to reinforce the English. Hepburn was killed, and his bravest knights were either slain or taken prisoner. This latter fate befell John and Thomas Halyburton of Dirleton, John and William Cockburn and Sir Robert Lauder of The Bass.[25] The date of his liberation does not appear to be on record but in 1405/6 he accepted Prince James into his safekeeping on The Bass, and there is a charter in "The Great Seal of Scotland" confirmed at Falkland in May 1411, which mentions Sir Robert de Lawedre, Knt., being 'present'. On the 15th June 1411 "Robertus Lawedyr, miles," had a *safe-conduct* from King Henry IV.

Not to be outdone or discouraged by these setbacks, Archibald, 4th Earl of Douglas, wishing to take advantage of the diversion of English arms to deal with the revolt of Owain Glyndwr in Wales, marched in August a second army as far as Newcastle, one of his leaders being Sir John Swinton of that Ilk, husband of Princess Margaret daughter of King Robert II. (The current Swinton of that Ilk is a Sir John who also had a military career.) The Percys again reacted forcefully, blocking Douglas's retreat near Homildon (now Humbleton) Hill near Wooler in Northumberland on the 14th September 1402.

---

[25] Balfour Sir James, *Annals,* vol.1; and Fordun's *Scotichronicon,* Edinburgh 1759.

Homildon

Though burdened with considerable loot, the Scottish army of just over 10,000 men was a formidable opponent, and the raiders were confident that their deployment on the slopes of the hill would be proof against an English advance. The Percys agreed, and the English men-at-arms stood back while their archers proceeded to decimate the Scottish ranks from a safe distance. When they could endure this galling fire no longer the Scots charged down the hill, only to find that although the archers retreated, their fire did not slacken.

Ballad singers tell us that Sir John Swinton (of Swinton) – "a doughty knight as ever Scotland bred" - and Adam Gordon of Gordon, another Berwickshire feudal baron, who had been mortal enemies up to now, became reconciled in this dire extremity and together led the Scottish nobility in a desperate effort to break through the English ranks:

Like two huge rocks on Braemar's brow,

60

When loosen'd from their bed,
That thunder down and overthrow
The pines that crown the glade.

Thus they, through ranks, the Earl of March,
And the bold Percies sought,
And blood and carnage mark'd their path,
Where'er they stept and fought.

At length they're wi' their gallant train,
By numbers compass'd round,
And fighting fall on heaps of slain,
And stain with gore the ground.

So did these valiant chieftains fall,
Who lived in mortal strife;
But lock'd In one another's arms,
Dear friendship closed their life.

The greatest slaughter took place on Red Riggs, the steep fields which lie to the west of the main road, and since then many skulls and bones have been turned up by the plough.

The Scots army disintegrated in flight, leaving seven prominent nobles killed and over eighty barons and knights captured. Douglas himself, despite losing an eye, and bearing the marks of five arrow wounds regardless of his coat of mail, was amongst the prisoners. Lord Percy, and George de Dunbar, 10th Earl of March, supporting the Northumbrians, wishing to follow up their successes, immediately assaulted Cocklaw Castle, the Gladstone stronghold near Hawick in Teviotdale, but the gallant garrison effectively resisted their attempts and obtained a truce.

Alan de Lawedre died shortly before March 1407 when his second son George, a Burgess of Edinburgh and husband of the daughter of Archibald 'The Grim', 3rd Earl of Douglas, was already designated "of Haltoun"[26]. An English Safe-coduct under the seal of the Lord

Chancellor was issued on 1st December 1412 till Pentecost following, for William, Sire de Graham, Master Robert de Lany, licensed in decrees and Provost of St. Andrews, William de Borthwick Esq., and George de Lawedre, Burgess, ambassadors appointed by the Council-General of Scotland to treat for the deliverance of James [1st] King of Scotland and for a truce, as signified in letters from the High Prince the Duke of Albany, the King's very dear cousin, with 40 horsemen in their company.[27] George de Lawedre was Provost of Edinburgh almost continually from 1413 to 1430 when he died.[28] He left four daughters, his co-heirs. The Haltoun estates passed to his brother and heir-of-entail, Sir Alexander de Lawedre, Kt., husband of Elizabeth, daughter of Sir John Forrester of Corstorphine, Lord Keeper of the Great Seal.

Sir Alexander de Lawedre of Haltoun joined his relative Archibald 4th Earl of Douglas, Duke of Touraine, with a large number of Douglas adherents including Sir John Forrester, in the great battle of Verneuil, in Normandy, on 17th August 1424, where Douglas led the French troops against the English under the Duke of Bedford. At the onslaught an altercation between Douglas and the French leader Narbonne as to precedence threw their troops into confusion, and a disastrous defeat was the result; the Earl of Douglas and his son James, Sir Alexander Lindsey, Robert Stewart, Sir John Swinton (whose father was killed at Homildon Hill) and two thousand others having been left dead on the field. The most vivid account of the battle is in Villaret's *Histoire de France*. The total loss of the allied Scottish, French and Italian army is generally computed at about 4000 men. Villaret said that the Scots bore the brunt of the battle. Sir Alexander survived, and died before June 1434. His son William, another Douglas adherent, succeeded his father at Haltoun.

---

[26] *The Great Seal of Scotland* Index 2 for July 1393, no.1686.
[27] Bain, Joseph, FSA Scot., editor, *Calendar of Documents relating to Scotland,* vol.iv, 1357-1509, Edinburgh, 1888, p.167, no.833.
[28] Whitson, Sir Thomas, LL.D., *The Lord Provosts of Edinburgh, 1296 – 1932* Edinburgh, 1932, p.3.

Chapter 4

JAMES I

In *The Stewartis Original,* a now lost work by John Barbour (c1320 - 1395), the author of the great epic poem *The Bruce,* Barbour traced the ancestry of the Stewarts back to Ninus, the legendary founder of Nineveh! These details can be gleaned from the Latin *Historia* by Hector Boece, published in 1526 and translated by John Bellenden in 1530. Other references to Barbour's work may be found in the *Original Chronical* by Andrew of Wyntoun.

There are several other stories as to the origins of this famous family, not least the one from Shakespeare's *Macbeth,* which, in an entirely fictitious scene, has Macbeth murdering Banquo (reputed Stewart ancestor) but failing to kill his son Fleance. Banquo also appears in Boece's *Historia.* Another highly imaginative yarn is that the Stewarts were descended from a hero who existed beyond the mythical Fergus, one Gaythelos, who had married Scota, daughter of the Pharaoh who ruled Egypt in the time of Moses.

However, the Shropshire historian, EW Eyton, writing in 1858, said correctly that Walter FitzAlan (the 1st) High Steward of Scotland until his death in 1177, had been brought to Scotland about 1136 by King David 1st from Shropshire. Walter was one of five brothers, sons of Alan FitzWalter (d.1153), Lord of Clun and Oswestry and a crusader, who in turn was the son of a man named Walter FitzFleald (d.1093), who was married to Christian, daughter of Alan 'Fergant', 4th Duke of Brittany. Eyton reached the apparently obvious conclusion that Fleance and Fleald must have been the same person.

FitzFleald, lt appears, owed his lands on the Welsh Marches to the favour of the English King Henry I, and it was at Henry's Court that David 1st must have made the acquaintance of Fleald's grandsons William and Walter. Sometime between 1136 and 1140, Walter became the High Steward of Scotland, taking over from Ailred of Rievaulx who had become a Cistercian novice after a visit to that famous abbey in north Yorkshire. Walter was given a grant of the feudal barony of Renfrew by the King. A few years later he founded the Paisley Abbey with Cluniac monks that he had brought to Scotland from the Priory of Much Wenlock in Shropshire. The Abbey was dedicated *for the souls of King Henry of England, King David and King Malcolm,* an endowment which provides a perfect illustration of the trans-national nature of many a feudal noble's loyalties.

James 5th High Steward (d.1309) a great-grandson of the above-- mentioned Walter, married Cecilia, daughter of Patrick, 5th Earl of Dunbar (killed in 1248 at the siege of Damietta, Egypt), and their son, the 6th High Steward, Walter "the Stewart", married Marjory, daughter of Robert 'The Bruce'.

Their son, Robert the Stewart, became Robert II, King of Scots on the death of King David II in 1371. I have already noted in the previous chapter, that Robert was in command of the left wing of the Scots' army at the Battle of Neville's Cross and, unlike his King, escaped.

At this point it might be pertinent to note that in the 14th century the Lauders were similar in status to the Stewarts and had been in Scotland prior to them. Robert the Stewart's father, Walter, was only knighted on the morning of the Battle of Bannockburn, whereas several Lauders had long held knighthoods. The historian Alexander Grant states: "The family of Lauder are recorded as amongst those below the rank of earl who have been considered as belonging to the Scottish higher nobility between 1325 and 1349".[29]

Robert II was crowned at Scone on the 26th March 1371. In 1336 Robert had married Elizabeth Mure of Rowallan, to whom he was related within the forbidden degrees of kinship, a situation which demanded that a Papal Dispensation be obtained before the marriage could be considered lawful. This situation was regularised in 1347

[29] Stringer, K.J., editor, *Essays on the Nobility of Medieval Scotland*, Edinburgh, 1985, pps: 214, 225, and 229.

64

when Robert tardily obtained the necessary Papal Dispensation therefore allowing him to name his first-born, John, Earl of Carrick, as heir to the throne. The Stewarts were thereafter able to maintain the line of succession in unbroken primogeniture until the birth of Mary, Queen of Scots in 1542.

Robert II died in 1390 and was succeeded by his eldest son, John, who took the name Robert III as the name John was considered unlucky. The Stewarts were prolific in conferring titles upon their kinsmen, evidenced by this King appointing his elder son David as Duke of Rothesay and upgrading the Earl of Fife (his brother), an earlier Stewart creation, as Duke of Albany. Robert III aged quickly and became semi-invalid. He was aware of his failures. The chronicler of the *Register of Moray* wrote:

"In those days there was no law in Scotland, but he who was stronger oppressed him who was weaker, and the whole kingdom was a den of thieves; murders, ravagings and fireraising, and all other missdeeds remained unpunished, and justice, as if outlawed, lay in exile outwith the bounds of the kingdom."

His reign saw a power struggle between Rothesay and Albany in which the King was little more that a helpless spectator. As anarchy spread Robert was persuaded, in 1401, to order Rothesay's arrest and the latter died in Falkland Castle the following year. Albany became the heir-presumptive. However, between him and the succession was his nephew, the King's younger son, now heir, Prince James, who had been born in 1394. Fearing Albany, Robert decided to send his surviving son to France, at the beginning of 1406.

The King, relying on the staunch loyalty of Sir Robert de Lawedre, whom His Majesty referred to as *our lovite of The Bass,* decided, meanwhile, to use Sir Robert's fortress as a temporary place of safety for the young Prince James until such times as a ship became available to convey him to France.

The following quotation from Wyntown's[1] *Cronykil* tells us the outline story of James' flight:

In-to the castell of the Bas
Oure Kingis Sone yeit bidand was,
His schip, a quihil fra this wes done,
Dis James oure Lord the Kingis Sone,
And wyth him of Ordinance
Of Orknay the Erle, to pas in France
And wyth him thare to be;
Few wes ordanyt ma Menye.
Bot yet he wes thare purvait wele
Of honest Clethlng, and Weschele
Of Silver bricht, and Jowelis ma
Our Prynce had wyth hym thare alswa.
And quhen he saw the Schip cum down
Fra Leith, he maid hym redy bown:
Wyth hym the Erle of Orknay, thare
And all the lave, that wyth thame were,
In-to that Schip thai maid Entre
In-till intent to pas the Se.

In March 1406, a ship of Danzig [where many thousands of Scots expatriates lived] named the *Maryenknight,* with the young James on board, weighed anchor off The Bass and sailed for France under cover of darkness. With him as guardian went Walter Wardlaw, Bishop of St Andrews, and Henry St. Clair, 2nd Earl of Orkney.

Sailing down the coast the ship was seized by English pirates off Flamborough Head on the 22nd March. Regardless of the truce that was then in force between the two countries, King Henry IV happily paid a miserable pittance for James and imprisoned the young boy in England for the next nineteen years, mostly in the Tower of London. The news of his son's capture added one last sorrow to the many

---

[1] Andrew of Wyntown (c 1350 - c 1425)

which bad afflicted "the most miserable of men" and Robert III died on the 4th April.

The Scottish Parliament recognised the imprisoned Prince as King James I. However, Albany now became Governor of Scotland in his absence. His son, Murdoch, had been a prisoner in England since 1402 and in 1416 Albany ransomed him for £10,000 leaving the King still a prisoner! In the course of Albany's governorship many enormities were committed in the Realm, perhaps the most memorable being a bloody battle long remembered as Red Harlan, fought near Aberdeen in 1411 between Donald, Lord of the Isles, who was Albany's nephew by his sister, and Alexander Stewart, Earl of Mar, also Albany's nephew by his brother! The occasion of the battle was a dispute concerning the Earldom of Ross, claimed by the Lord of the Isles; it was not, as it has often been called, a clash between Highland Lowland cultures.

Under Robert III a great dispute such as this could be submitted to judicial combat, but under Albany's governorship, the solution was private war. Albany's younger son John, Earl of Buchan, then took a force of 7000 men to France in 1419 and defeated the English at the battle of Bauge in 1421. Albany meanwhile had died the previous year and in 1422 Henry V of England also passed away. The English Regency Council acting on behalf of King Henry Vl was eager to prevent the Scots from further fighting with the enemy, France, and accordingly opened negotiations upon those terms for the release of King James 1st.

William de Lawedre, Bishop of Glasgow and Lord Chancellor of Scotland (eldest son & heir of Sir Robert Lauder of The Bass[30] – not Alan, as has been claimed), and his younger brother Sir Robert de Lawedre of Edrington (and later The Bass)(d.1451), with George de Dunbar, 10th (and last Dunbar) Earl of March, and others, were sent by Murdoc, Duke of Albany, to England to treat concerning James's liberation, according to a *Safe Conduct* dated the 19th August 1423. This was successful and on the 10th September 1423 the Scots agreed

---

[30] *Registrum Glasguense*, vol.2, p.304. National Records of Scotland.

to pay £40,000 sterling. One of the seven seals appended to this treaty is that of Sir Robert de Lawedre. James de Lawedre (Sir Robert's jnr's brother), Justice-Clerk South of the Forth, is included in the party of the Earl of Angus, Hepburn of Hailes, Hay of Yester, etc., in another *Safe-conduct* dated December 13th "to come to the presence of the King of Scotland at the city of Durham".

On the 3rd February 1424 Henry VI sealed *Safe-conducts* for a number of nobles to proceed to the city of Durham as hostages for the diliverance of King James. This included "Robert de Lawedre of The Bass, knight, with 18 servants" and his son James, the Justice-Clerk, with four servants. That was followed by a treaty of indenture dated 28th March between King James and the nine English Ambassadors agreeing to a truce for seven years from 1st May following; neither the King nor his subjects to assist the enemies of the other; and an obligagtion by James to pay £40,000 sterling the King of England.

In a subsequent *Safe Conduct* granted "for diplomatic purposes", by King Henry VI, *Robertus de Lawdre de Bass, Chivaler,* and his son James, are both mentioned as being responsible for escorting James I back to Scotland, after agreeing a ransom of 60,000 marks.

Tytler says that in 1425 "the Earl of Mar, his son Sir Thomas Stewart, William Lauder Bishop of Glasgow and Chancellor, Sir Walter Ogilvy the Treasurer, John Cameron Provost of the Collegiate Church of Lincluden and private secretary to the King, Sir John Forrester of Corstorphine Chamberlain [father-in-law of Sir Alexander de Lawedre of Haltoun], Sir John Stewart and Sir Robert Lauder of the The Bass, Thomas Somerville of Carnwarth, and Alexander Livingston of Callender, all members of the King's Council, were the only persons who King James admitted to his confidence, and entrusted with the execution of his designs".

James 1st had not been inactive whilst in captivity and decided to ally himself with the powerful Douglas Family. In November 1412 he issued letters confirming Sir (later Earl) William Douglas of

Drumlanrig, and his brother Archibald, in their lands of Drumlanrig, Hawick, Selkirk and Cavers.

It appeared to James 1st that Albany's son, Murdoc, was plotting a coup d'etat and in 1424 he was arrested along with his wife, their son Alexander and Murdoch's father-in-law, Duncan, Earl of Lennox. King James consigned to the Lauder's Castle of The Bass Walter Stewart, the eldest son of Murdoc. The person who received the payments for the prisoner's support was Sir Robert de Lawedre. In 1425 John Herring was Constable of the castle on the Bass for Sir Robert. Also arrested with them was Sir Robert Graham of Kincardine, who escaped nursing an implacable hatred for his King. Murdoch's other son James, who remained at liberty, then burnt Dumbarton and murdered Sir John Stewart, the King's uncle. As a result, in May, Murdoch, his sons Walter and Alexander and the Earl of Lennox were all beheaded at Stirling Castle following a trial by 21 noblemen, with the Earl of Athol as the foreman of the assize.

In 1426 James I, in his parliamentary reforms, enacted that all tenants-in-chief of the King - prelates, earls, barons and freeholders - were to attend future parliaments and General Councils in person in order to make parliament more representative, particularly by including the minor barons along with the great feudatories. Meanwhile, other alliances were being made too, and the final deliberations regarding the marriage of Sir Alexander Home of that Ilk (later 1st Lord Home) to Marion Lauder (granddaughter of Sir Robert Lauder of The Bass) were sealed by Robert, Bishop of Caithness at Edinburgh on the 1st April 1428. The Bishop procured the use of the [Lauder of The Bass] seal of George Lauder, Bishop of Argyll, his own not being available, before witnesses led by Sir Robert Lauder, Knt., Lord of Edrington. This Sir Robert was Governor of Edinburgh Castle from 1425 to 1433, when he was replaced by Sir William Crichton of that Ilk, another robust lowlander.

Further efforts by James 1st to implant law and order and kingly authority in Scotland were evidenced in 1428 when he summoned fifty Highland chiefs to a council at Inverness Castle, and there threw them into a prison. However, on this occasion only three were executed. James was annoyed that Highland men commonly robbed and slew one another and he intended to put a stop to all this by making an example of the Chiefs. But in a fierce spirit of defiance, Alexander, Lord of the Isles, son of that lord who had been defeated at Harlaw, gathered an army of 10,000 men and burnt Inverness. James acted immediately and marched into Lochaver on the 23rd June 1429 inflicting a total defeat upon the Lord of the Isles, who subsequently spent a short spell of imprisonment in the Douglas's Tantallon Castle, opposite The Bass.

In 1427 Charles VII of France had proposed a new alliance with Scotland: marriage between his son the Dauphin Louis, and James's eldest daughter Margaret, whose dowry should be a force of six thousand soldiers rather than money. James accepted the French proposal, one of whose ambassadors had been Sir John Stewart of Darnley, *Sieur d'Aubigny,* a distinguished soldier and the founder of a famous Franco-Scottish family. The Treaty was signed at Perth by James, and by the King of France at Chinon, in November 1428.

As a result of these Scottish reinforcements (against the English) Joan of Arc was able, it might be argued, to achieve far more than if they had not been available, as the Scots did much of the hard fighting under her. An English fleet was sent out to intercept the ships which were carrying Margaret and her entourage to France, in May 1436. Although unsuccessful, James, perhaps enraged as much by his own memories as by the attempted seizure of his daughter, laid a hasty and ineffective siege to Berwick. An English invasion followed, but the invading force was defeated by a Scots army under the Earl of Angus at Piperden in Berwickshire.

Foiled before Berwick, James turned his attention to Roxburgh, a Scottish fortress which was long in English possession. However Queen Joan arrived with news of a conspiracy in Edinburgh led by the aforementioned Sir Robert Graham of Kincardine, and James abandoned the siege.

Thinking he had subsequently settled the disputes by negotiation the King spent Christmas in the Dominican Priory at Perth. On the night of the 20th February 1437 the King and Queen retired after he had spent most of the evening playing chess. Into the quietness and tranquillity of the Priory, Sir Robert Stewart, Master of Athol, who was also Chamberlain, admitted the still unsatisfied conspirators: Sir Robert Graham and his son Sir John, Thomas Hall, and Christopher and Thomas Chambers, burgesses of Perth. Walter of Stratoun, a servant of the King, met the armed men outside the Kings chamber, recognised their purpose, shouted "treason!" and was slain.

Given the warning, the King and Queen and her ladies tore up floorboards to break a way through into the vault beneath the chamber, the only hiding place. The King was no longer the athletic young man he had been. The murderers finally burst in, wounded the Queen as she struggled vainly to hold them off, and located the King's hiding place. Unarmed and encumbered by his gown, he fought for his life with his bare hands. He was left dead "with twenty eight wounds, most towards the heart". One of the murderers was killed by Patrick Dunbar of Cockburn who came, too late, to the King's aid. The rest escaped that night but all were captured within the month. All were executed, Graham and Athol enduring three days of torture with *burning iron* prior to their end.

King James II was crowned on the 25th March 1437. He was aged six. The minority of James II was another period of disorder, but not of anarchy, with Archibald, 5th Earl of Douglas being appointed as Guardian of the Realm. The rise of the Douglases, like that of the Stewarts in earlier centuries, had been gradual, and had been connected with good service to the crown, the first Earl of Douglas being a nephew of Sir James Douglas, a supporter of Robert 'The Bruce'. This firm loyalty was now to change.

In 1439 William Douglas sent Sir Robert Lauder's son John (some refer to him as Alan, John's uncle) who was married Anna, daughter of Patrick Hepburn, younger, of Hailes (who fell at the Battle of Nesbit Moor), as an ambassador to the French Court, accompanied by

Sir Malcolm Fleming of Cumbernauld, to do homage for the Duchy of Touraine, coveted by Earl William. In this mission they were successful.

However, the Douglases were said to be scheming against their king and shortly after their return to Scotland, the Earl of Douglas, who was not yet eighteen years of age, and his brother David, a lad of twelve, were inveigled to Edinburgh Castle by Chancellor Crichton under pretence of being made companions to their youthful sovereign King James II, then only eight years old; and there they were treacherously put to death without trial or warning.

Speechless with astonishment, the brothers were bound, led out to the courtyard of the castle, and beheaded, in spite of the imploring tears of the young King, to whose retributive account, however, in after years, this crime was laid. Four days later, Sir Malcolm Fleming shared the same fate, but it is recorded that *Alane* de Lawedre escaped, probably through the intervention of his kinsman, Thomas Lauder, Bishop of Dunkeld.

Chapter 5

MURDERS AND DISCONTENT

William, 8th Earl of Douglas, had established a potentially treasonable connection with Richard, Duke of York, the father of the future Edward IV of England. In France, after a pilgrimage to Rome in 1450-51, Douglas sought but failed, to obtain the restoration to his family of the Dukedom of Touraine. Abercromby writes, in his *Martial Achievements,* "thither the Earl of Douglas went and with him his second brother James, as also the lords Hamilton, Gray, Seton, Salton, Oliphant, Forbes, Urquhart of Cromarty, Fraser of Philorth, *Lawder of Bass*, Campbel, Calder etc. These noblemen and gentlemen were so very numerous and so well equipped, that as they made a very noble figure in their passage through Flanders and France, so they filled even Rome itself with the expectation of their arrival".

James II, now of age, took advantage of Douglas' absence to establish his authority (Douglas was summoned to appear in judgement by the King who accused him of flagrant acts of misused power while in office as Lord Lieutenant) with a year of vigorous activity. Serious violent disturbances broke out in the Douglas territories, which had been left in the care of the Earl's youngest brother, Sir John Douglas of Balveny, who appeared to lack authority but in fact was encouraging the Earl's vassals to rebel. James quelled them by seizing and destroying a number of Douglas strongholds. At this point John, Lord of the Isles & Earl of Ross, in support of the Douglases, sacked Inverness (again!). James quelled this rebellion also without difficulty.

Stories of these rebellions "reached the ears of the Scots pilgrims at Rome" so that many of the Earl's followers deserted his standard. The Earl, concerned for himself and his friends, obtained from King Henry VI on his return to England (en-route to Scotland) a *safe-conduct* promising them protection and safety within King Henry's territories during the space of three years.

Besides his own name, and that of his brother Sir James, we find Sir James Hamilton, Sir Alexander Home, Sir William Cranstoun, Sir Nicholas Campbel, John Clark, Andrew Gray, *Sir Willian Lauder of Halton*, Thomas Cranstoun, Andrew Kerr, Charles Murray, George Haliburton, John Doddes, John Greenlaw, George Finlaw, Alan Lawder (presumably Alan Lauder of that Ilk who died after October 1464) and James Bishop. However, Douglas had far too much ambition to remain in England for any length of time and we find him back in Scotland within a year.

Gradually the King discovered the means by which the Earl was building up his power: intrigues with the Yorkists in England and a league with the Lord of the Isles and Alexander Lindsay, the new Earl of Crawford. James, according to an old chronicle, ordered Sir William Lauder of Haltoun to be his messenger in 1452 when the King summoned Douglas to Stirling Castle. Douglas had recently incurred the King's further resentment by putting to death, in the cruellest manner, Lord Colville, Sir John Herries, Sir John Sandilands of Calder, and particularly Maclellan, called the 'Tutor of Bomby', ancestors of the Earls of Kirkcudbright. Mclellan's crime was to refuse to join the Earl's league against his sovereign.

Sir William Lauder was a close and trusted friend of Douglas and witnessed a great many of his charters, including one signed at Edinburgh on the 26th January 1451/2, the year of action. Tytler also relates how King "James despatched Sir William Lauder of Haltoun, who had attended Douglas in his pilgrimage to Rome, with a message to him , expressive of the desire of the King to enter into a personal conference, promising absolute security for his person". Douglas therefore accompanied Sir William Lauder back to Stirling Castle where he was graciously received by the King on February 22nd. But violent arguments developed after dinner and the King, angry that the Earl refused to return to his former loyalty to the Crown, drew his dagger and struck the Earl in the throat. Sir Patrick Gray intervened and struck the Earl upon the head with a poleaxe. Then several others of the King's bodyguard also stabbed him until the corpse was covered with twenty-six wounds. His body was then thrown from the window into the privy garden below and subsequently buried there.

Nationwide conflagration followed. The Bishop of Aberdeen, one of the dead Earl's brothers, rode into Stirling at the head of several hundred men and burnt the town. The Douglases accused Sir William Lauder of being the King's accomplice and Haltoun castle, which was then a fortified L-shaped Tower, was immediately besieged by the Douglases and taken; but it was eventually recaptured by the Lauders with the King's aid, he sending a large supply of ammunition and men to their assistance. It is even stated that the great *bombard* which was placed on four carts and drawn by a large number of horses, sent by the King, was none other than the famous *Mons Meg*. There is no doubt whatever about the expense of this coming to the rescue of Haltoun being paid by the State, for we read in the Chamberlain Rolls of an account being rendered in 1453 at the Exchequer, for the hire as well of men as of horses at Haltoun in the time of the siege of the same; and for iron caps, called salattis, given to the servants and archers of the King, and for pitch, bitumen, and carts of the carriage of divers beams, and for wages and expenses of masons and carpenters present at the Tower of Haltoun. However, the greatly wronged Sir William Lauder was killed in the defence.

In May the Earl of Crawford, leading a rebellion in the north, was defeated near Brechin by the first Earl of Huntly. James himself, with 30,000 men, marched on the new Earl of Douglas who surrendered near Dumfries. Parliament had already conveniently exonerated the King from the murder, and James, 9th Earl of Douglas, was obliged to formally forgive his Sovereign. In return the King settled upon him the Earldom of Wigtown.

Douglas, however, nursed his enmity, though for a time he concealed it. In 1455 the Douglases rose again against James II, but finally, at the bloody battle of Arkinholm, were utterly defeated. Their two greatest strongholds, Abercorn in West Lothian and Threave in Kirkcudbrightshire were reduced by the latest addition to the King's armoury - enormous pieces of artillery, the newest development of military science. *Mons Meg*, James' masterpiece, had a range of two miles and required 105 lbs of gunpowder to fire it.

James II now created new semi-honorific Earldoms, which possessed no great territorial endowments, but which bound the recipients in bonds of obligation to the Crown. This was his way of ensuring loyalty and nipping in the bud any future rebellious conspiracies. He married his sister Annabella to the victorious Earl of Huntly and gave the Earldom of Athol to his half-brother John Stewart. The Earldom of Morton was bestowed upon a loyal Douglas, Sir James Douglas of Dalkieth, to whom the King married his dumb sister, the Princess Joan. Hay of Errol, the Constable of Scotland, was created Earl of Errol in 1452. From this reign also date the Earldoms of Argyll, Marischal and Rothes; the early medieval Earldoms having become vested in the Crown, either by reversion or annexation.

At this point the question must be pondered - what of the Lauders, one of the Crown's most loyal families, whose steadfast support to every true monarch was unswerving? Surely they should have received honours placing them far ahead of those whose loyalty was doubtful and needed to be bought? We will see how some of the new peers, many with unearned titles, were later found unreliable following the Union of Crowns in 1603 and thereafter, particularly during the Great Civil War, which finally led to the extinction of Scottish sovereignty.

In 1447, the truce with England, well-kept in recent years, expired, and the following spring there was an outbreak of Border warfare. In May the English burnt Dumfries, and the Scots burnt Warkworth. Hugh Douglas was the victor in a more serious engagement in October when he defeated an English invasion at the Battle of Sark, near Lochmaben. The occupied town of Berwick was now surrendered by Henry VI of England to James II of Scotland. About 1460 Berwick Castle was put into the hands of Robert Lauder of Edrington, son and heir of The Bass, who kept his position

76

uninterruptedly till 1474. For this charge, Lauder received 200 marks per annum. He retired that year and was succeeded by David, Earl of Crawford for just under 2 years, before being reappointed yet again.

Sir Robert Lauder of The Bass, was noted as being present in Parliament in 1471, 1478, 1481, 1483, and in 1488 was on a Parliamentary Committee.[31] The Lord of Bass is mentioned as one of the barons who were responsible in 1469/70 for the administration of justice in Civil Causes before the erection of the College of Justice.[32]

On 2nd February 1477, King James advised the bearers of the instalment of Princess Cecilia's dower that he had sent, amongst others, Robert Lauder of Edrington, son and heir apparent to Robert Lauder of The Bass, to conduct them to Edinburgh.[33] This Sir Robert Lauder, *fils*, of Edrington, and after his father's death in 1495 of The Bass, married Isobel, second daughter of John, 1st Lord Hay of Yester. Robert had at least two sisters: Katherine, who married Sir John Swinton of that Ilk and Isabella, who married Alexander Leslie of Warderis.

I shall digress here to discuss the castle and Lauder estate of Edrington, 5 miles from Berwick-upon-Tweed, which the Lauder if the Bass family held from before 1300 (then from the Bishops of Durham). "Edrington Castle, opposite Paxton, was once a place of great strength and importance"[34] "Towards the close of the 18th century Edrington was still four storeys in height, a commanding ruin perched on the pinnacle of a crag clothed in trees. On the western side the castle was inaccessible and was well adapted to stem the torrent of incursions from the English shores of the Tweed".[35]
"The ancient castle occupied the summit of a steep bank above the Whitadder, and must have been a place of considerable strength and importance. It was burnt by the Duke of Gloucester's army in July

[31] *General Index to the Acts of Parliaments of Scotland,* Edinburgh 1875.
[32] *Acts of the Lords of Council in Civil Causes*, vol.ii, 1496-1501, p.xcviii.
[33] Bain, 1888,vol.iv, no.1445, p.294.
[34] Maxwell, Sir Herbert. *The Story of the Tweed*, 1909.
[35] Gould, H. Drummond, *Brave Borderland*, 1934.

1482 but was soon afterwards rebuilt and fortified by order of the Scottish Parliament. Later again captured by the English, in 1546 the Scots demanded that their "house" of Edrington should be immediately restored to them; and in accordance with a treaty concluded in the church at Norham, Edward VI delivered it up.[36] Holinshed said that "as often as it was taken in war (by the English) it was delivered again at the making of peace".

After the Union Edrington Castle fell into decay. Gould adds that "it has suffered more from the attentions of local vandals [stone thieves] than it ever did from the English" while Maxwell laments that it "has been quarried away to near ground level". Notwithstanding this, Edrington Castle still appears on modern Ordnance Survey maps. After being a Lauder possession for four centuries, the Edrington estate was sold in the 17th century to cadets of the Scott of Clerkington family, a daughter of whom was married to Richard Lauder, laird of Haltoun. At the close of that century it was purchased by John Douglas DD, son of Douglas of Parkhead and a brother of Lord Mordington. Interestingly the 4th Lord Mordington was married to a Catherine Lauder. Edrington estate forms the lower half of the parish of Mordington.

In 1460 Henry VI of England was captured by the Yorkists at the battle of Northampton and carried a prisoner to London. His Queen, Margaret de Anjou, and their son Prince Edward, made their way to Scotland seeking help and refuge. James's Queen, Marie de Gueldres, agreed to provide Margaret with a supply of Scotland's ever-plentiful commodity - fighting men. James II, ostensibly an ally of Henry VI against the Yorkists, saw the wars of the Roses in England as an opportunity to recover those 'Scottish' possessions which remained in English hands.

Upon receiving news of the battle of Northampton of July 10th, James advanced to Roxburgh and laid siege to the castle, which was held by its governor, Lord Faucomberge, who had commanded the vanguard

---

[36] Mack, James Logan, *The Border Line,* 1926.

of the Yorkist army at Northampton. (This was William de Neville, 8th son of the Earl of Westmorland. Interestingly, his wife Joan was a daughter of Sir Thomas Faucomberge of Skelton Castle, and a descendant of the de Brus of Skelton family, the ancestors of Robert 'The Bruce'.) There, on the 3rd August, the Scottish King met his death when standing next to one of his beloved artillery pieces; it exploded, the force of the explosion instantaneously killing him.

His Queen, Marie, accompanied by the nine year old heir, continued the siege and Roxbugh Castle fell: the King's death had not been in vain! On the 10th August the young heir was escorted from Roxburgh to the nearby Abbey of Kelso where his coronation as King James III then took place.

Queen Margaret of England had meanwhile returned to England and rallied her forces and, at the battle of Wakefield on the 30th December, 1460, inflicted a crushing defeat upon the Yorkists. After the battle, the Duke of York was decapitated and his head set above the city gates of York. His son, Edward, Earl of March, declared himself King Edward IV, and then pursued the Lancastrians northwards, utterly defeating Henry VI's army at the battle of Towton (where again Lord Faucomberge commanded the Yorkists) on the 29th March 1461. Henry, Margaret and the Prince of Wales, along with the Duke of Somerset, escaped north to Newcastle-upon-Tyne.

In June 1461 the Lancastrians under Henry VI and the government of James III of Scotland concluded an offensive alliance and besieged Carlisle and then moved on to threaten Durham. However this assault petered out, the reasons being unclear. Certainly by September Alnwick castle was in the hands of Edward's followers, and in June the Scots Queen Mary made a truce at Carlisle with the Earl of Warwick.

In 1476 we find King James III granting letters to Robert Lauder of Edrington appointing him *Keeper of the Castle of Berwic-upon-Tweed* for the next five years. In *The Exchequer Rolls of Scotland* under Account of the Bailiffs and Chamberlains of Berwick, 1478, a payment is made to the said Robert de Lawder of Edrington for the repair of the gates of Berwick castle and the restoration of the roofs of various houses in that castle on the King's order, Alexander Leslie de Warderis the Receiver-general, attesting the order on the account, £50. (Lauder's daughter Isabella was married to Leslie). Patrick Hepburn, 1st Lord Hailes took over from Lauder in 1481 but was forced to surrender to the English in just under a year on the 25th August, 1482, the final year of Scottish occupation.

Five years previous to this, King James III had appointed Alexander, Lord Home, Sir Adam Blackadder of that Ilk and Sir Robert Lawder of Edrington *sonne and apperande are til our loveit Robert Lawder of the Bass* to conduct to Edinburgh from the English Court, 2000 marks (£22,000) as an instalment to Edward IV's daughter Cecilia's dowry.[37] She had been betrothed as a child to the young Prince James, Duke of Rothesay, in 1474. However, in 1479, James III broke this treaty of marriage, leading to a renewal of the wars which had been relatively dormant. The Duke of Albany appears once more on the scene at this point, declaring himself *Alexander of Scotland, by the gift of the King of England,* at Fotheringay Castle on the 10th June, 1482. He promised that if he were placed upon the throne of Scotland by English aid, he would acknowledge Edward IV as his overlord, terminate the alliance with France and make no other alliances without Edward's leave, and surrender to England Berwick, Lochmaben, Eskdale and Annandale.

In addition he agreed to divorce his wife and marry the Princess Cecilia himself, and that if he could not obtain such divorce he would marry his heir to an English bride. Upon these disgraceful terms he was provided with an English army commanded by Edward's brother, Richard, Duke of Gloucester (the future King Richard III). Together, Albany and Gloucester marched north to lay siege to Berwick.

In July James mustered his army on the Burgh Muir of Edinburgh, and marched down Lauderdale to encounter the invaders and relieve

---

[37] Bain, vol. iv, 1888, no.1445.

Berwick. James had placed Robert Cochrane, his architect and a Royal favourite, as his Master of the Artillery. The King had been experiencing periods of unpopularity of late, particularly because he had a number of favourites who were detested by the nobles. One was Cochrane, who was said to be terrifically arrogant. When he received a grant of the lands which had previously belonged to the King's other unfortunate brother, the Earl of Mar, who had died in mysterious circumstances in the Preston's Craigmillar Castle, disaffection increased.

The Lauder burgh *auld kirk,* now completely demolished, stood about sixty yards in front of Lauder Fort (now completely rebuilt as Thirlestane Castle). In this *auld kirk* the disaffected of James III's nobles met after the King's army had encamped nearby. This gathering included the Earl of Angus, the Earl of Buchan (the King's uncle), the Earls of Douglas, Huntly, Crawford and Lennox, and Lord Gray. The trend of the discussion was that the favourites were insufferable, and that something ought to be done.

Oliver Lauder of that Ilk (a descendant of The Bass), then Deputy Sheriff of Berwickshire and who resided up the hill in his Tower, had refused the conspirators permission to meet in the Royal Burgh of Lauder's Tolbooth even though he had been told that it was to be a Council of War. Forewarned, he intimated a reluctance to be in any way involved and suggested they meet elsewhere. Fortunately for Oliver (who died in 1489), the conspirators gracefully accepted his rebuttal and withdrew to the *auld kirk* where four centuries of Lauders were then buried including two bishops, one being William (d.1425) a Lord Chancellor of Scotland. One may suppose that the Lauders were on the King's side of the quarrel.

Cochrane suddenly appeared at the kirk and this brought matters to a climax. Heaping insults upon him, the disaffected Lords arrested Cochrane and rushed to the King's pavilion to seize the other five, their 'national crimes' augmented in the eyes of the great nobles of that chivalrous age by the fact that not one of them was really a *gentleman* in name, mind or manners. The only one among them whose father had been knighted was young John Ramsay of Balmain, whom James had showered with honours, who now clung to the King, who put his arm around him and begged for his life from the stern Douglas. He was to survive the night, as was James Hommyl, the King's tailor. The King was 'escorted' to Lauder Bridge to witness the execution by hanging of Cochrane and the others. However, the King slipped away and was later captured in a house on the main street of Lauder which, we are told in *The Grange of St. Giles,* was still standing in the latter decades of the 19th. Century.

Instead of marching south against the English, the 50,000 strong army returned with the Lords to Edinburgh castle, with the King as their prisoner. John Ramsay of Balmain (who later fell at Flodden) was permitted to accompany him and to remain in the castle where the King was placed under "a gentle and respectful degree of restraint", under the care of his uncles, Athol and Buchan.

Albany, the King's brother, was still besieging Berwick-upon-Tweed which, meanwhile, had fallen to the English.. The Scottish Lords were, at that stage, unaware of Albany's traitorous secret agreement at Fotheringay Castle. However, it seems probable that Angus and Gray knew of it, in view of their subsequent behaviour. Archbishop Scheves, the new Bishop of Dunkeld[38], Archibald Campbell, 2nd Earl of Argyll (another who fell at Flodden) and the Chancellor Lord Avondale were empowered to treat with Albany on the King's behalf. Meanwhile, the powerful Burgesses of Edinburgh were demanding the King's release. Leaving the Duke of Gloucester to reduce Berwick, Albany accompanied the negotiators to Edinburgh and even joined his voice to those of the citizens in demanding the release of the King.

On the 25th. September the King emerged from the castle, where he had been a prisoner since the end of July. To illustrate his

---

[38] Thomas Lauder, Bishop of Dunkeld, had died on 4 Nov 1481. He was an illegitimate son of Sir Robert de Lawedre of The Bass, &c. Thomas had been continually engaged in the service of James Ist and 2nd, Kings of the Scots, and was tutor James II in his minority.

reconciliation with his brother he rode downhill to the Abbey of Holyrood with Albany sitting behind him on the same horse. No-one seems to have given a thought, meanwhile, to the poor garrison and burghers of Berwick.

After the reconciliation James kept Albany perpetually at his side; he caused him to accompany him everywhere, eat at his table and even share his bed! On December 11th Albany was appointed Lieutenant of the Kingdom and entrusted with its defence. This may have been James' way "to shame him by trusting him". Albany betrayed that trust and inaugurated the year 1483 by sending Archibald, Earl of Angus and Andrew, Lord Gray to England to reaffirm on his behalf the agreement of Fotheringay, and to promise King Edward IV the allegiance of them all.

This was formalised in a Treaty signed at Westminster between the English Crown's Commissioners, led by Henry, Earl of Northumberland, on February 11th, and Lords Angus, Gray & Sir James Liddle for Albany, which stated that "The Duke of Albany, on obtaining the Scottish Crown, and on his death, his commissioners, renounce their allegiance to Scotland, and become the liegemen of England; he will dissolve the league with France, and assist the King of England to its final conquest – assist James, Earl of Douglas to recover his estates according to the convention between the Earl of Angus and him (Douglas?); and will take one of the King's daughters in marriage without any charge to him. In consideration of which offers the King of England undertakes to assist the Duke to the conquest of the crown of Scotland."

Comings and goings between Scotland and England, however, were always liable to discovery, and within a matter of a few weeks Albany's new treason was divulged to the King. One of these 'leaks' was a letter from George Cely, a merchant of Calais, to an Englishman of rank at Naples giving an account of the Duke of Albany's swearing fealty to the King of England, and his proposed expedition to Scotland with a force of 60,000. On March 19th Albany was dismissed from his Lieutenancy of the Kingdom of Scotland and he and his supporters were forbidden to come within six miles of the King. Albany went south to England once again, admitting an English force to the castle of Dunbar on the way (it was still in English hands in September 1484).

On the 2nd June Albany was declared a traitor, forfeit in life, lands and goods. But fortune had already deserted Albany, for on the 9th April his patron Edward IV had died. A power struggle developed as a result and Albany's ambitions mattered little to those involved. The English boy-King Edward V and his younger brother disappeared in controversial circumstances, with the Duke of Gloucester first becoming Protector and then King Richard III.

However, Albany still had a friend in England: the long-exiled James, 9th Earl of Douglas. In a desperate venture, backed by only five hundred men, Albany and Douglas invaded Scotland in July 1484 by the western route, burnt Dumfries, and attacked Lochmaben Castle. But it was the time of the annual fair and the town was crowded. The little force was routed and though Albany escaped, Douglas was taken prisoner. He was brought before the King, upon whom it is said that he turned his back. Douglas, who had lost one brother to the dagger of James III, two to the executioner's axe and one on the battlefield, could not have been expected to love the Stewarts, even though the fault lay with the power-hungry and often traitorous Douglases in the first place. The King showed his customary mercy and Douglas was ordered to spend the rest of his life as an inmate of Lindores Abbey. Albany, however, fled first to England and thence to France where, in 1485, he was accidentally killed by a splinter of a lance as he sat as a spectator at a tournament.

In 1484 yet another truce was concluded between England and Scotland. However, Richard III of England's position was threatened by the Lancastrian claimant Henry Tudor, and on the 22nd August 1485 at the Battle of Bosworth Field, Richard met his death.

It was now requested by the new King Henry VII that Edward IV's widow, Elizabeth Woodville, who was once again restored to legitimacy, would marry James III whose wife, Margaret of Denmark, had died in July 1486. It was also agreed that James's second son, James, would marry Katherine, third daughter of the late King Edward IV. The Truce dated 3rd July also stated "the castle and town of Berwick to remain neutral."

In 1486 Pope Innocent VIII had sent to Scotland as Papal Legate the Bishop of Imola, who brought James the Golden Rose, the symbolic gift yearly presented to the ruler whom the Pope deemed to be the most faithful son of the Church. Unfortunately the Legate also brought a stern religious inquisitional-type brief with him to make certain that the sanctions of the Church were applied to the unruly unsparingly.

Herein lay the roots of the future conflicts and the end of Scotland as a Roman Catholic country. The Church in Scotland was particularly rotten with corruption and nepotism and despised by the nobles and peasantry alike. The former partly because they coveted the Church's vast estates and wealth, and the latter because of the Church's oppression notably through the tithe system whereby 10% of their valuable crops had to be given to the ecclesiastical authorities, usually the great Abbeys.

A row, for instance, had developed over James III's annexation of the revenues of Coldingham Priory to finance a double choir for the Chapel Royal of Stirling. Coldingham Priory had been a cell of the Benedictine Abbey of Durham and its community of English monks was unwelcome in Scotland as it provided a centre for espionage. As a result the Berwickshire Homes, a famous feuding family, expelled them and took possession of Coldingham for themselves. One of the Homes was then in the Church in Rome and had proposed himself as Provost of the Priory. However, he died in 1478 and James III persuaded Pope Innocent VIII to permit him to suppress the almost non-functioning Priory altogether.

The Homes were, not unnaturally, enraged, and they participated vigorously in the rebellion which led to the King's down-fall. Familiar names appeared again amongst the rebel Lords, led by Angus. With him were Gray, [Hepburn of] Hailes, Argyll and Lyle. The King's party was not unimpressive, containing the Earls of Huntly, Glencairn, Bothwell, Errol and Athol, and the Earl of Crawford recently created Duke of Montrose; Archbishop Scheves and Bishop Elphinstone. Also there were Ruthven, Drummond, Sir Alexander Lauder of Haltoun and Lord Semphill.

On the 2nd February 1488, the Keeper of Stirling Castle handed over the King's young son Prince James to the rebels. An agreement, the *Pacification of Blackness,* clearly with the King under duress, was arrived at, for a Regency,

This truce was broken and on the 11th June 1488 the King and the rebels met at the Battle of Sauchie Burn, in sight of Stirling castle. The King was mounted on a "great grey charger" which served him well in the flight that was to follow the rout of the King's forces. But the King was thrown from his horse during that flight and injured. He was rescued by miller Beaton and taken to his Mill at Sauchie, the miller being unaware of the King's identity. James announced who he was and promptly asked for a priest. The miller's wife brought a man who said he was a priest back to the mill. The man, whose identity has never been discovered, *drew his dagger and 'gif him four or fyve straikis ewin to the hart.* Pitscottie declared that some believed the King's murderer to have been a servant of Lord Gray, named Borthwick, who with Gray had pursued the King closely. James III was buried beside his Queen, Margaret of Denmark in the Abbey of Cambuskenneth. He was only 36 years old.

A Petition to Pope Innocent the Eighth signed in the presence of Henry Congleton and others in 1488, craved absolution for numerous people during the *recent troubles* in Scotland and also refers to the battle of Sauchie. Amongst those named the first is Robert Lauder (d. before Feb 1508) "son and heir apparent of the Lord of Bass and

Baron of Stenton, &c." Others included Kentigern Hepburn of Waughton[39], Patrick Skowgale[40], Alexander Sidserf[41], William Sinclair, David Renton of Billie[42], Alexander Home, Archibald Dunbar[43], William Manderston, Gavin Hume[44], and John Sommerville, all Lowlanders.[45]

James III had recovered Dunbar Castle and during the last years of his reign he was driving a hard bargain with Henry VII for the restoration of Berwick. But with his death in 1488 the position of Berwick remained anomalous. The town or borough, to its outermost limits, remains to this day in England, detached from its county of Berwickshire and so from Scotland. The reign of James concluded in violence. Under him law and order were areas of neglect, and the only areas of success were to be found in foreign affairs. He mistakenly created his favourite survivor of the massacre at Lauder Bridge, John Ramsay, Lord Bothwell. Dreadfully ostentatious, Ramsay earned himself the hatred of many and this title was, after the King's murder, annulled by Parliament. Ramsay then fell at Flodden.

---

[39] Married to Margaret, daughter of SirRobert Lauder of The Bass, &c., which Robert died before February 1508.
[40] Patrick Scougal of that Ilk was a close friend of Sir Robert Lauder of The Bass, who witnessed a charter of Patrick's on 26 Sept 1504.
[41] Who fell at Flodden. His son Patrick was married to Jonette, daughter of Sir Robert Lauder of The Bass, &c., which Robert died before February 1519.
[42] Married to Elizabeth, daughter of Robert Lauder of The Bass, &c., (which Robert died in 1495) by Jonette, daughter of 1st Lord Home.
[43] Archibald Dunbar of Beil. On the 10th July 1498 an action was raised by Sir Robert Lauder of Bass, Knight, as assignee to the deceased David Dunbar of Beil, heir of the deceased Alexander Dunbar of Beil. See: *Acts of the Lords of Council in Civil Causes, 1496 - 1501*, volume ii, page 261.
[44] Presumably Gavin Hume of Wester Spott, Captain of Tantallon Castle & son of Alexander Home of Polwarth by his first wife, Margaret Crichton. Alexander's third wife (Gavin's stepmother) was Margaret, née Lauder, widow of Kentigern Hepburn.
[45] The Historic Manuscripts Commission - *Report on the MSS of Colonel David Milne Home of Wedderburn Castle*, London, 1902, p.263-4, number 606.

An essay by Alexander Grant entitled "Extinction of Direct Male Lines" mentions that the Lauders were one of only 31% of the great families of the time of Robert the Bruce who survived in the direct male line beyond 1500.[46]

---

[46] Stringer, ed., 1985, p.214.
88

Chapter 6

FLODDEN

James IV was fifteen years old when the murder of his father made him King of Scots. He felt forever guilty about his father's death and vowed that he would refuse absolution, even if it were offered by the Pope. He was crowned at Scone on the 26th June 1488. John Ramsay, Earl of Bothwell, was later deprived of his title which was then conferred upon Patrick Hepburn, 2nd Lord Hailes, then Sheriff of Berwickshire. (Hailes Castle is near East Linton in East Lothian). Several others made their peace with the new King. The vanquished, who could have won the battle but lost with the coronation of the dead King's son, were generally treated with moderation and thus did not scruple to take advantage of their position.

Lord Home, a leader in the rebellion, assumed the office of Great Chamberlain, and also became Warden of the East March, baillie of Ettrick Forest, Keeper of the castles of Stirling and Newark, Steward of the Earldom of Mar and Guardian of one of the King's brothers! Lord Hailes, besides becoming Earl of Bothwell, was appointed Master of the Household, Warden of the West and Middle Marches, Keeper of Edinburgh Castle and Guardian of the second of the Princes. Angus became the official Guardian of the King.

Nervous at the turn of events in Scotland on 19th July 1488 a Crown Commission was signed at Westminster "for array and muster for the defence of the town and castle of Berwick and parts adjoining Scotland, all the able hobelars and archers there, and in the castles of Norham, Bewcastle, and Carlisle; also to supervise the artillery and munitions of war within the fortifications of those places." A three-year Truce was subsequently signed by Henry VII's Commissioners and the Scots at Coldstream on the 5th October.

In 1489, the Earl of Lennox, and Lords Lyle and Forbes, to whom the new regime had not made itself acceptable, raised an army in rebellion which was speedily crushed, their respective castles being reduced by the Royal artillery. James IV nevertheless pardoned them and restored their privileges and titles to them after a brief period of forfeiture.

Anglo-Scottish suspicion had also increased that rebellious year and Sir Andrew Wood, with two ships, the *Yellow Carvel* and the *Flower*, captured five English vessels, which were privateering in Scottish waters. Three further English ships then attempted, with Henry VII's encouragement, another foray off the Isle of Mey where a great sea fight took place and once again the Scots were victorious.

In April 1491 King Henry VII entered into an agreement with John Ramsay, the Earl of Buchan, and Sir Thomas Tod of Sereshaw, for the kidnapping of James IV and his next brother the Duke of Ross. They received £266-13-4 on loan, which was to be repaid if their plot miscarried, as indeed it did. Another mutilated document also reveals that Angus had promised, upon certain conditions, to hand over the great Border stronghold of Hermitage Castle in Liddesdale to Henry VII. This latter act of treachery was discovered and Angus was warded in his own castle of Tantallon, on the headland opposite The Bass. Hermitage Castle was given to the new Earl of Bothwell. In late 1491 another five year truce was signed between England and Scotland.

During the last decade of the fifteenth century numerous rebellions of a fierce yet local nature took place in the northern Isles and north-western Highlands, all of which were dealt with effectively by James IV.

In the middle of the 1490s Anglo-Scottish relations became complicated by the arrival in Scotland of Perkin Warbeck, a pretender to the English throne who enjoyed the support of Margaret, Duchess of Burgundy, the sister of Edward IV and widow of Charles the Rash. Warbeck, a Fleming of obscure origin, claimed that he was Richard, Duke of York, the younger brother of Edward V. Edward and Richard, the "Princes in the Tower" had disappeared at the beginning of the reign of Richard III in mysterious circumstances. Their fate to this day is a complete mystery although it is generally accepted that they were murdered in the Tower. Margaret of Burgundy had been the real Richard's aunt. In 1494 Margaret requested James IV to receive her nephew 'the Prince of England'. In 1495 Warbeck arrived and was magnificently received at Stirling. James, with characteristic generosity, made him an allowance of £1,200 (presumably Scots' pounds!) a year and permitted him to marry Lady Katherine Gordon, the daughter of the Earl of Huntly.

The question of Berwick remained uppermost in Scottish minds as it remained in the hands of Henry VII. This 'Richard of York' promised to cede it back to Scotland in return for Scottish help in securing his throne

War was subsequently declared in September 1496. The pretender was proclaimed Richard IV, and James invaded northern England with a small army, inviting 'King Richard's' subjects to rally to his support. Their response was negligible. The Wars of the Roses were a not too distant memory and their was no enthusiasm for yet another Civil War. The army withdrew. Hostilities were renewed by the spring of 1497 but there was little serious fighting, for by this time James was disillusioned with the political possibilities of the pretender. Another Anglo-Scottish truce was negotiated in 1497 and on the 6th July Warbeck left Scotland, with his wife, by sea. He later invaded Cornwall but was captured, confessed to being an imposter, and was imprisoned in the Tower where he was executed in 1499.

In 1497 King James IV visited his loyal servant Sir Robert Lauder in his castle on The Bass.[47] The boatmen who conveyed him from Dunbar were paid 14 shillings.[48]

In 1498 Henry VII proposed that James IV should marry his eldest daughter the Princess Margaret Tudor. Because they were jointly related through the Beauforts, a Papal dispensation was obtained by

---

[47] Reid, 1885.
[48] Phillimore, R.P., *North Berwick, Gullane, Aberlady and East Linton District*, North Berwick, 1913, p.50.

Henry in 1500 permitting such a union. James, however, had a mistress, Margaret Drummond, whom he loved deeply. Matters became clearer however when in 1500 Margaret and her two sisters died of poisoning immediately after breakfast in their father's castle and were buried by the grief-stricken king in the cathedral of Dunblane.

In October 1501 James at last reluctantly accepted Henry's offer of the hand of his daughter. A "firm treaty of peace" was then negotiated, with a Papal confirmation. James was 30 and Margaret 13 years of age. She arrived at Dalkeith Castle on the 3rd August 1503 where James visited her that evening. They were married at Holyrood on the 8th August. Margaret bore James IV six children, of whom only one survived, the son born in 1512 who would succeed his father aged just 1 year.

James IV's reign was notable for the imposition of Law and Order and for the tight administration of civil justice. He was co-founder of the University of Aberdeen in 1495, the first university in the British Isles to have a faculty of medicine. He also initiated what has been claimed as the first compulsory education act. In 1507, under the King's auspices, Messrs. Chepman and Myllar set up Scotland's first printing press in Edinburgh. Also, the College of Surgeons was founded in 1506.

On the 16th January 1508/9, at Edinburgh, Sir Robert Lauder of the Bass, knight, was made Captain and Keeper of the King's castle and fort of Lochmaben, with all pertinentes and numerous other privileges.[49] His wife Elizabeth was a daughter of Richard Lawsone of Hieriggs, Lord Justice Clerk to the King.

It was, however, a period of great upheaval in Europe, one of alliances and kings attempting to affect the balance of power. In this respect, Louis XII of France was the rising power and others sought to curtail

[49] Livingstone, M., I.S.O., editor, *The Register of the Privy Seal of Scotland*, vol.1, 1488-1529, Edinburgh, 1908, no.1799, pps: 273/274.

France's ascendancy, notably the Holy League of Spain, The Pope, Venice, England and the Holy Roman Emperor Maximilian.

Henry VIII, the new English King, was desirous of glory and still hopeful of regaining some part of England's medieval empire in France. James IV of Scotland endeavoured until the last to assist Louis Xll by diplomacy rather than by sword. On the 26th July 1511, a Safe-Conduct was issued by King Henry VIII to the Earl of Argyll, Lord Drummond, Sir Robert Lauder, Sir William Scott, Sir John Ramsay and Mr. James Henderson, Ambassadors from Scotland, to come to England to negotiate a treaty. [50] However things continued to deteriorate. On 6th December 1512, King James IV wrote a letter from Holyrood Palace to King Henry VIII of England, in which the Scottish monarch craves a safe-conduct for Scottish Commissioners John, Lord Drummond, Robert Lauder of the Bass, John Ramsay of Trarenzeane and William Scott of Balweary, *knights*, and Master James Henryson, Clerk of Justiciary, to meet the English Commissioners to discuss redress and reparation for attacks by sea.[51]

In March 1513 Sir Robert Lauder of The Bass was re-appointed to the command of Lochmaben Castle for a further period of 7 years, a post he appears to have held until his death (before Feb 1519).[52] His being in command of it probably saved him from the slaughter at Flodden in 1513.

However, on the 5th April 1513 Henry concluded the Treaty of Malines with the Emperor Maximilian, which bound both of them to attack France, Scotland's ally. On the 18th April Ferdinand of Spain also entered the Treaty. Their action committed James to war with England. At the end of June Henry VIII invaded France and James IV's principal herald visited him in his camp at Calais with an

---

[50] Thorpe, M.J., editor, *Calendar of State Papers Relating to Scotland* vol.1, 1509-1589, London, 1858. Also in *The Letters of James the Fourth 1505-1513*, p.208, where he is described as "Sir Robert Lauder of The Bass".
[51] Hannay, Robert Kerr, LL.D., editor, *The Letters of James the Fourth, 1505 – 1513* Edinburgh, 1953, no. 496, pps: 274/5, and p.286.
[52] *Register of the Privy Seal of Scotland,* vol.1, no.2383.

ultimatum. Henry sent him packing. On the 16th August Henry VIII defeated the French at Guinegate and French pressure was now brought to bear upon the King of the Scots to relieve the French by drawing English troops back to England. One week later, on the 22nd August, James IV invaded England "desite the counsel and remonstrances of his veteran officers and nobles", and proceeded to reduce the English castles of Norham, Wark, Etal and Ford, which served the double purpose of safeguarding his line of retreat, and of drawing northward the army which had been left to defend England which was commanded by the septuagenarian Thomas Howard, Earl of Surrey.

In the meantime James's fleet, headed by the *Great Michael,* under the command of the Earl of Arran, sailed to the assistance of the French King. Unhappily, the naval half of the enterprise was hopelessly mismanaged by Arran, and worse still the best of James's gunners had sailed with him, thus reducing the efficiency of the Scottish artillery which would encounter Surrey.

Because of the feudal system Scotland did not possess a standing army and there were very considerable logistical problems with such a hastily organised army of this size – up to, it is said, some 40,000 men. It was therefore accompanied by a contingent of French soldiers who had been serving as military advisors to the Scots, improving their tactics and teaching the use of the 18 foot Swiss pike. In addition a field force of 5000 French troops was present under the command of the Comte d'Aussi.

Norham Castle fell on the 27th August and during the fourteen days the army spent in siege operations there was already a steady reduction in its strength through desertion and sickness. David Smurthwaite, writing in his *Battlefields of Britain*, argues that at this stage there had not been time to weld the army of Highlanders, men from the Isles, Lowlanders and Borderers into a cohesive fighting force able to stand the strains of battle.

In contrast the English army and its plans for the defence of the north had been preparing since the end of June. Surrey ordered a general muster at Newcastle-upon-Tyne for September 1st. Nearly 26,000 men assembled and Surrey marched them northwards to Alnwick where he was joined by his son Thomas, the Lord Admiral, with 1200 men from the English fleet. At Alnwick, Surrey organised his bowmen and billmen into an effective command structure and summoned a Council of War to discuss the coming campaign.

Norham Castle

Worried that the Scots might retreat across the border prematurely Surrey issued a challenge to James in which he offered battle by Friday 9th September at the latest. James accepted, and the English army moved confidently forward expecting to meet the Scots on the plain of Milfield on the 7th September.

As he prepared for action, however, Surrey received the disturbing intelligence that the Scots had marched westwards and deployed in a formidable position on the Flodden Edge, near Branxton, a hill rising to a height of 500 feet and over a mile in length, with its right flank protected by marshy ground and its left by a precipitous slope. The only feasible approach along the road which traversed the centre of the hill was covered by Scottish artillery. The only solution that appeared open to the English was to envelop the Scots via the eastern flank and attack from the rear.

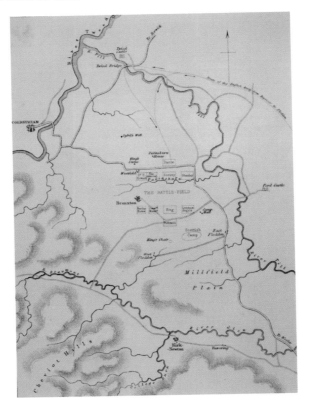

Flodden

At dawn on the 8th September the English Army marched north for 6 miles in lashing rain until they came to Barmoor Wood. The next day they pushed on towards the bridge at Twizel. The vanguard under the Admiral crossed to the west bank of the Till via the bridge, while the rearguard under Surrey forded the river at Milford. The Scots were

96

puzzled by this English manoeuvre and at first they did nothing to counter it. On the 9th, however, they received firm intelligence that the enemy had crossed the Twill at Twizell and a stormy Council of War finally decided that the army should move to Branxton Hill, a mile to the north of Flodden Edge. With some difficulty James and his nobles turned the army around and marched north to the new position.

On the Scottish left were the Borderers and the Highlanders under Lord Home and the Earl of Huntly; with Sir Alexander Lauder of Blyth, Provost of Edinburgh and Justice Depute, and his brother James Lauder of Burngrange[1] amongst others in the mounted division. In the centre were the troops of the Earls of Errol, Crawford and Montrose with the King's column to their right, and on the extreme right the Highlanders and Islanders under the Earls of Argyll and Lennox.

The Scots' reserves were the French troops and the men of Lothian under Adam Hepburn, 2nd Earl of Bothwell who also had with him Sir George Lauder of Haltoun, elder brother of the two already mentioned.

The action began with an artillery duel in which the English established a clear superiority, and although the casualties inflicted must have been few, the bombardment unsettled the Scottish infantry, particularly on the left wing.

Here the Borderers suddenly swept forward down the hill and crashed into the Cheshire levies under young Howard who gave way after a short resistance. The Scottish centre troops were ordered forward to support the Borderers and as they closed on the English line they were raked by cannon and volleys of arrows. Errol, Crawford and

---

[1] Mr A Thomson, writing in *Lauder and Lauderdale* (1902) states that "on the right bank of Lauder Burn, and a few hundred yards from its junction with the River Leader, has stood for many generations a building locally known as the Burn-Mill, but more properly the Burngrange". Attached to this building were certain lands and the package gave James Lauder the designation "of Burngrange".

Montrose's divisions made little impact but the king's column pushed Surrey's men back over 300 yards. While the English centre was fighting to maintain its position, Cumberland's Lord Dacre led 1500 cavalry against the victorious Borderers who instead of continuing the battle were busy plundering the dead. Fighting almost ceased in this part of the field as a result. But on the extreme left Sir Edward Stanley was about to enter the battle.

Attacking up the eastern slope his archers poured a devastating fire into Argyll & Lennox's troops, and the Highlanders, not wishing to wait for the English charge disappeared from the field. (Writing in *Goodbye to All That*, Robert Graves states, somewhat controversially, that nothing much had changed even in World War I, where, he says, Highland Scottish Regiments took unnecessary risks in the trenches, had unnecessary casualties, and without officers were useless).

At the foot of the hill d'Aussi's and Bothwell's troops were being crushed by weight of numbers. Stanley's men, their business on the crest of the hill now over, crashed into the rear of the King's division. The English pikemen had proved their worth by constantly standing their ground when attacked by the Scots, and the bill had proved its worth throughout the battle.

James fought throughout the battle, often right up in front, but he was pierced firstly by an arrow and then mortally wounded in the head by **a** bill-hook, within a few paces of the Earl of Surrey, At the crisis of the battle Alexander, 3rd Lord Home refused to come to the King's assistance saying "He does well that does for himself. We have foughten our vanguards, and have won the same, therefore let the lame do their part as well as we." (He survived the battle but was executed 3 years later). Then, joined by the mosstroopers of Tynedale and Teviotdale, his men too stripped the slain and plundered the baggage of *both* armies. The battle lasted from half-past four in the afternoon and continued until nightfall when the carnage was halted as darkness separated the combatants.

The return to Edinburgh of a Flodden survivor

Having lost their King, and almost all their nobility, the remnants of
the army silently retreated across the border. Scotland lost James, and
his son the Archbishop of St.Andrews, two bishops, two mitred
abbots, twelve Earls, thirteen titled lords, five eldest sons of peers,
fifty knights and chiefs, "a member of every leading family in the
land", and of *gentlemen* **a** number uncalculated; in all over 10,000
Scots lost their lives on that fatal field. The Haltoun branch of the
Lauders was almost extinguished at Flodden with the deaths being
recorded of Sir George Lauder, *the laird of Halton,* and his two

brothers James, of Burngrange, and Sir Alexander Lauder of Blythe, Provost of Edinburgh. The English losses were no more than 1,500, with few of those men of note.

Scottish power, as it was, for the time being, was utterly broken. It is said that Henry VIII petitioned the Pope to have James IV buried in St Paul's Cathedral. However, nothing seems to have happened and his resting place remains a mystery. But John Stow, the Elizabethan annalist and antiquary, wrote in his *Survey of London,* in his description of the church of St Michael's, Wood Street:

"There is also (but without any outward monument) the head of James IV, King of Scots of that name, slain at Flodden Field, and buried here by this occasion; after the battle the body of the said King being found, was enclosed in lead and conveyed from thence to London, and so to the monastery of Skene in Surrey, where it remained for a time ... I have been shewn the same body so lapped in lead... thrown into a waste room amongst the old timber, lead and other rubble. Since which time workmen there, for their foolish pleasure, hewed off his head; and Launcelot Young, master glazier to Her Majesty (Elizabeth 1), feeling a sweet savour to come from thence, and seeing the same dried from all moisture, and yet the torm remaining with the heir of the head and beard red, brought it to London to his house in Wood Street, where for a time he kept it for its sweetness, but in the end caused the sexton of that church to bury it among other bones taken out of their charnel."

Chapter 7

PINKIE

King James V of Scotland had been born on the 10th April 1512, and therefore at the time of his accession was only seventeen months old. . Ten days after the Battle of Flodden, the Lords of Council, at Stirling Castle, on the 19th September 1513, set up a Regency Council of the Realm "to sit upon the daily council for all matters occuring in the realm" of 35 Lords (15spiritual the rest temporal, etc.), amongst whom was [Sir Robert Lauder, Knt.,] "The Laird of Bass", on behalf of the Dowager Queen[53], he who had been Governor of Lochmaben Castle.

The new King's coronation took place in the Chapel Royal of Stirling on the 21st September 1513, with Queen Margaret Tudor, his mother, as Regent, in concert with the abovementioned council. This was a curious arrangement given that she was the devoted sister of the King whose army had been victorious at Flodden.

John, Duke of Albany, the son of James III's traitorous brother by his French Duchess, had been born and brought up in France and was to all effects a Frenchman; but he was not altogether unknown in Scotland, for James IV had corresponded with him and had occasionally employed him as an agent in his foreign diplomacy. Those members of the nobility and clergy who were opposed to the rule of Margaret Tudor advocated dismissal of the Regency Council and alternatively the appointment of the Duke of Albany as Regent. A letter of invitation from them was duly despatched to him before the end of 1513.

In order to maintain her position, Margaret was forced to rely increasingly upon the pro-English House of Douglas and in August 1514 the Queen married the young head of that house, Archibald, 6th Earl of Angus.

---

[53] .Hannay, R.K., editor, *Acts of the Lords of Council in Public Affairs 1501-1554*, Edinburgh, 1932.

Albany arrived in Scotland in May 1515 and was ceremonially installed as Regent on the 10th July. As Margaret had remarried her regency was, technically, forfeit. Upon his installation as Regent, Albany at first sought an alliance with Queen Margaret, but she, understandably, received him as an enemy. He was well aware that without either the friendship of the Queen Mother or the custody of the King and his infant brother, his authority would remain a dead letter.

Therefore in August 1515 Albany besieged Queen Margaret in Stirling Castle and demanded the custody of the Royal Children. Defeated, Margaret was escorted to Edinburgh Castle. She did not see James again for almost two years and her younger son she never saw again, for he died a few months later. Margaret, with the help of the English Lord Dacre, then fled with Angus to England where she gave birth to the only child of her second marriage, Lady Margaret Douglas, destined to become the mother of Lord Darnley, the ill-fated consort of Mary, Queen of Scots.

The Berwickshire Home family had, in the meantime, been conspiring with Henry VIII and Queen Margaret, and in 1516 rose in rebellion against Albany. The rebellion was, however, quelled, and Lord Home and his brother were tried and executed in the autumn for treason. Sir William Lauder of Haltoun, whose father fell at Flodden, was a close supporter of John, Duke of Albany, and in 1515 the Duke granted Sir William a licence to "refortify and re-edify his house at Haltoun." During the minority of James V, Scotland was in a continuous state of internal dissension and party strife; the very streets of Edinburgh were filled with the brawlings and mortal combats between the powerful houses of Angus and Arran, or the Earls of Huntly, Moray and Home. The Lauders of the two main families were frequently mixed up in these quarrels, hence the need for Sir William to strengthen his castle near Ratho. Sir William is also on record as a knight of St John of Jerusalem.

James V

On the 2nd June 1517 "The Laird of Bass" [Sir Robert Lauder of The Bass, &c., who died before Feb 1518/19] was one of the twenty one new appointments as a Lord of Session for all of Scotland.[54]

I shall divert briefly here with an interesting story of one of Albany's unfortunate appointees. At Broomhouse, near Duns, Berwickshire, where once stood a tower house, there was at one time a cairn marking the grave of Sir Anthony d'Arcy, Sieur de la Bastie, a French knight whom the Regent had appointed Warden of the Marches in place of Alexander, 3rd Lord Home who, with his brother, had been executed. As it was believed that de la Bastie had brought this about, David Home of Wedderburn attacked him near Langton, outside Duns, on the 12th October 1517, routed his party, and pursued him over the moor of Duns, where the French knight's horse got bogged. De la Bastie tried to escape on foot, but Home was too quick for him; he

---

[54] Hannay, 1932, p.93.

rode him down, cut off his head, bore it in triumph through the streets of Duns, and later fastened it aloft on the battlements of the still extant Hume Castle.

Duns Castle, in 1320 a seat of the Moray family and subsequently much fought over by invaders

In 1517, whilst in France, Albany was temporarily detained by a new Anglo-French alliance. During his absence the order which he had imposed in Scotland speedily collapsed. The principal agents of disorder were the Earls of Angus and Arran. Angus, as the husband of Queen Margaret, sought supreme power through the pursuit of a pro-English policy. Arran, as the Premier nobleman in Albany's absence, found the pretensions of Angus intolerable and sought to counter them by a pro-French policy. The ensuing power struggle culminated in a street battle in Edinburgh in the spring of 1520, in which the Douglases were victorious. Margaret returned to Scotland. However,

104

by 1519, she was secretly planning to secure a divorce from Angus so that supreme power would be vested in her.

The brittle alliance of Henry VIII and Francis I collapsed shortly after their famous meeting at the Field of Cloth of Gold, and in 1521, Albany returned to Scotland. Henry formed a new alliance with the Holy Roman Emperor Charles V, which committed them to a concerted attack upon France. Francis had accordingly sent Albany back to Scotland to arrange a Scottish invasion of England, the traditional form of support which the Kings of France expected under the terms of the *auld alliance.*

As the noble Duke of Albany was related by marriage to the family of Pope Clement VII, Albany discovered, upon his arrival back in Scotland, that he had a new supporter – Queen Margaret, who sought to use Albany's connections to obtain her divorce. However, when Albany organised a military expedition against England in July 1522, Margaret's English patriotism took hold and she betrayed the Duke's plans to Lord Dacre. Also, it was widely known that, after Flodden, the Scots were reluctant to once again take to the field on behalf of an ungrateful ally, as Albany soon discovered. Dacre offered a temporary truce and Albany thankfully accepted.

However, in September 1523, after spending another year in France, Albany returned to Scotland with French reinforcements. Meanwhile, Henry VIII had offered his daughter Mary as a bride for James V.

His offer was refused and as a result an English army burnt Kelso and Jedburgh. Anti-English feelings were once again aroused and Albany's latest invasion proposals were now more acceptable. But after besieging Wark Castle, the onset of winter weather and the heralded approach of an English army forced him to retreat. In the spring of 1524 Albany left Scotland for the last time, his reputation damaged by two inglorious military expeditions.

Taking advantage of his departure, Queen Margaret, assisted by Arran, regained control of the King and with it her position as Head of

State. In the summer of 1524 Margaret and Arran declared the twelve-year-old King to have attained his majority. Albany's regency was formally terminated. Yet Margaret was not at all popular and her position was extremely insecure. Surprisingly, Henry VIII suddenly gave his support to the divorced Angus ("better than five Earls of Arran") who returned from exile. Margaret was forced to accept Angus as a member of her re-established Regency Council, over which he quickly gained an ascendancy. In November 1525, he initiated a *coup d'etat* after which James V remained a virtual prisoner of the Douglas faction until 1528.

Meanwhile, Henry VIII managed to obtain from Pope Clement VII his sister's divorce. In 1526 she married, for the third time, Henry Stewart, younger son of Lord Avondale. Subsequently, James V created him Lord Methven. Robert Lauder (d.1576) appears to have been under threat as on the 2nd January 1526 "the Lord of The Bass" was one of those (with friends) who the Duke of Arran signed a bond not to harm.

From ancient charters we know that the Lauders of The Bass, and also of Haltoun, were not only involved in all these conspiracies, but retained huge estates. In the Great Seal we find Robert Lauder of that Ilk (a cadet of Bass) granting to his eldest son, Robert Lauder (who had married Alison, daughter of John Cranstoun of that Ilk) and his heirs, his lands of the Forest of Lauder, with half of the Mill of Lauder, his lands in Dalcoif (at Mertoun), with tenants etc. This Charter was confirmed by James V on the 11th January 1525, one of the witnesses being Richard Maitland of Lethington (today Lennoxlove) of the Lauderdale family. Robert Lauder of that Ilk (senior) was by the end of that year, however, in temporary difficulties.. He appeared in person before the Lords of Council on 1st December stating that in 1518 he had incurred such substantial losses due to Border raids and incursions that he had still not recovered and was now seeking protection from his creditors.[55]

---

[55] Hannay, 1932, p.232.

Elsewhere, we find Henry Lauder, grandson of Sir George who fell at Flodden, "our Lovit familiar Clerk" being appointed in 1533 as Deputy King's Advocate to James V. Five years later Henry was appointed full Lord Advocate, and was also one of the first seven judges authorised by Parliament in the first erection and institution of the College of Justice, styled Lord St Germains.[56]

King James V was educated by Gavin Dunbar, later to become Archbishop of Glasgow and Chancellor. James had an insatiable desire for stories, with tales of King Arthur, Hector, Alexander, Pompey and Julius Caesar, Hercules and Sampson, all heroes for the King to emulate. He also learnt Latin and French. His education ended, however, with his mother's coup. He was only twelve. His only significant achievements noted after that were his expert horsemanship, and martial sports, in which he excelled. During the regime of Angus, James was separated from the household which had served him all his life, and became surrounded by men whom he came to regard as his enemies.

During 1526 James developed an attachment to John Stewart, the Earl of Lennox. James appealed to Lennox to help him regain his liberty, and the first plot, to snatch the King from the Douglases while Angus and James were attending a Justice Ayre on the Border, was a failure.

In August 1526 Lennox left the Court, and from Stirling issued a general appeal to the nobility of Scotland to assist in rescuing the King. An overwhelming response followed, including Margaret and her husband, the Archbishop of St Andrews, the Earls of Argyll, Moray, Cassillis and Glencairn to a good representative selection of the lesser nobility. The Lauders and The Bass and Haltoun were among them. There is a Respite by James V to William Lauder of Haltoun and others for their assistance to George Lord Home and umquhile David Home of Wedderburn, rebels, dated 28th May, 1527.[57]

---

[56] Dalrymple of Hailes, Bt., Sir David, *An Historical Account of the Senators of the College of Justice of Scotland from its Institution*, Edinburgh, 1849, p.63.
[57] National Records of Scotland. GD135/1062.

On the 4th September 1526 Angus led his army out of Edinburgh and commanded his brother, Sir George Douglas, to follow as quickly as possible with the King. lt was a black day for James.

In the battle, which took place near Linlithgow, the King's would-be rescuers were defeated and scattered, and Lennox was murdered after he had surrendered. In triumph the Douglases brought the King to Stirling, still their captive. After Linlithgow, Arran again withdrew his support, which meant that the Douglas regime was not supported by a single member of the greater nobility.

Numerous though the Douglases were, Angus had not enough kinsmen to staff the entire administration. He was forced to rely upon the services of careerists from baronial families, such as Henry Lauder, later Lord St.Germains. They were undoubtedly secretly loyal to James and this was, ultimately, to benefit both themselves and the King in the future.

The King escaped during the last days of May 1528. According to Pitscottie James escaped from Falkland during the absence of Angus, Kilspindie and Sir George Douglas who had left James Douglas of Parkhead in charge of the King. The Douglases quickly gathered at Falkland and rode in pursuit, but as they drew near to Stirling they were met by a herald with a proclamation which forbade them to approach within six miles of the King. There, at Stirling, less than two months after his sixteenth birthday, James V began his personal rule.

Angus retired to and defended himself in Tantallon Castle, that famous Douglas stronghold opposite The Bass, and it was November before he surrendered and withdrew with his principal kinsmen to England, where he was received favourably by Henry VIII. In December, when a five years' peace was signed between Scotland and England, it was agreed that Angus should permitted to reside at the English Court. Douglas family history was repeating itself.

Although the "Laird of The Bass" was with the King on 10 Oct 1528[58], it is also clear from Pitcairn's *Ancient Criminal Trials in Scotland*[59], that some kind of minor friendship had remained between the Lauders and their ancient compatriots the Douglases, as on the 7th April 1529 "Remission was given to Robert Lauder of The Bass and others for treasonably intercommuning, resetting and assisting Archibald, Earl of Angus, George Douglas his brother, and Archibald their uncle".

Just before the surrender of the Douglases, James made the first of his ruthless attempts to bring law and order to Scotland, starting with the Highlands. On the 10th November 1528 he issued *Letters of Fire and Sword* to his half-brother, the Earl of Moray, by which he, with the assistance of four other Lords, was commanded to exterminate the notoriously disorderly Clan Chatten, sparing only priests, and women and children, who were to be deported and set ashore on the coasts of Shetland and Norway.

In 1529 & 1530 James gave his attention to the borders. In 1529 he captured and executed the well-known freebooters, Scott of Tushielaw and Cockburn of Henderland. In 1530 the King mounted an expedition to Liddesdale where he captured the notorious marauder John Armstrong of Gilnockie, who was also put to death. Armstrong was one of the more infamous Border Reivers. It appears that the lauders were otherwise occupied in these border operations as the same year, in a list of Barons and Lairds of Berwickshire, Robert Lauder of that Ilk is noted amongst them, were being summoned, on 18th May for neglecting their bonds regarding suppressing Border thieves.[60] Very soon, order was restored throughout Scotland.

However, in 1539, Donald Gorm of Sleat, in the Isles, rose in rebellion and laid claim to the Lordship of the Isles. The rebellion was abortive. However, in 1540, the King made a circumnavigation of the north, visiting Orkney and the Western Isles, and took prisoners and

---

[58] Hannay, 1932, p.288.
[59] Edinburgh, 1833.
[60] Pitcairn, Robert, *Ancient Criminal Trials in Scotland,* Edinburgh, 1833, vol.1, p.146-7.

hostages from several clans whose loyalty he doubted. He also brought home with him a number of Chief's sons for education at Court. Upon his return, he finally annexed the Lordship of the Isles to the Crown.

New taxes were also imposed and the already mentioned College of Justice established. But more disturbing was the 1532 Act of Parliament by which James resolved "to defend the authority, liberty, and freedom of the seat of Rome and halikirk" (ie., the Holy Church). This followed the 1525 Act forbidding the importation of Lutheran books. For some years the dissemination of Lutheran ideas had been relegated as a threat to the orthodoxy of the Roman church in Scotland. *Extracta e variis cronicis Scocie* records Master John Lauder, an illegitimate son of Sir Robert Lauder of The Bass (d. bef. Feb 1508), was Archdeacon of Tweeddale and Teviotdale and, more importantly, Secretary to the notorious Cardinal Beaton, he like Beaton fought the Reformation with vigour and was responsible, as Scotland's Public Accuser of Heretics, for the prosecution of many heretics, including, notably, George Wishart the martyr in 1546 (see appendix).

On the 1st January 1537 James V married the frail Princess Madeleine of France at the cathedral of Notre Dame in Paris. This was regardless of the fact that he had been a positive rake with a trail of mistresses and illegitimate children in Scotland. By Margaret, daughter of Lord Erskine, for instance, he had a son called James Stewart who, as Earl of Moray, would later play a prominent part in Scottish power politics. Poor Madeleine died on the 7th July, 1537, just two months after her arrival in Scotland and was buried in Holyrood Abbey.

James remarried in the summer of 1538, another French bride, Mary de Guise, widow of the Duc de Longueville. The 17th July, it is recorded, was the "entrie of the Quenes Grace" to Edinburgh. Gilbert Lauder, burgess, and his son Henry, Lord St Germains, were delegated to welcome Her Majesty to Edinburgh: "it is deuysit for the honour of the Kingis Grace and the guid towne at the entry of owre Souerane, that thair be...... Gilbert Lawder in tanny (aray in gownis of veluott)" and "it is devysit that Master Henry Lauder, King's Advocate, be the persoun to welcum the Quenis Grace in sic abulyement, and with words in Frensche, as sall be devysit with avyse of Maister Adame Otterburne, Maister James Fowlis and David Lyndsay".

James' harsh dealings with his nobility were, by 1537, earning him few friends. The misdeeds of Angus appeared to be forgotten and the exiled Douglases were even pitied in some quarters as victims of Royal oppression! James returned from France, (with Madeleine), to discover that during his absence his mother had been attempting to negotiate a divorce from Lord Methven, with a view to being reunited with Angus! The King was uncompromising and quashed the divorce proceedings, ordering Margaret to return to Lord Methven. She died in 1541, still bitter.

Several others were condemned to death for 'treasonably conspiring', sometimes on the flimsiest of evidence. Amongst them were John, Master of Forbes and Angus' brother-in-law, and Lady Glamis. The latter, a great beauty, was burnt at the stake. The severity of the measures did not assist the King's popularity crisis. So alienated were the nobility *en bloc* that a foreign ambassador observed that of the greater nobility, not one was a member of the King's Council, which consisted of "none else but the papistical clergy".

The influence of Queen Mary de Guise and Cardinal Beaton provided an additional source of strength to James's already strong personal commitment to the *auld alliance* and the Roman Catholic Church. Yet the Beatons were, in reality, renaissance politicians in Holy Orders. Cardinal Beaton typified what was least praiseworthy in the clergy of the period by leading a life that was openly non-celibate. He was admittedly a great scholar who had studied at the universities of Glasgow, St.Andrews and Orleans; but learning was no longer typical of most of his Scottish contemporaries.

Possibly the most shocking example of episcopal ignorance was provided by Bishop Crichton of Dunkeld, who cheerfully admitted to an apostate priest on trial before him in 1539 that he had never read either the Old or the New Testament. "And yet," he said, "thou seest I have come on indifferently well." Regrettably, the lower clergy was no better.

The churchmen of Scotland may not, indeed, have been intrinsically worse than their counterparts in the rest of Europe; but the realisation was slow in reaching them that, in order to combat Protestantism, they must put their house in order. Whilst James V was aware of the need for reform he himself was party to the abuses. He had persuaded Pope Paul III to appoint his bastard sons as Commendators, or titular Abbots, of six of the richest abbeys and priories in Scotland, Kelso and Melrose among them, the revenues of which were consequently diverted to the Crown.

By 1540 religious matters were becoming a problem for James V. Henry VIII also sent Sir Ralph Sadler to Scotland with instructions to urge James upon the road to reform. Many of the Scottish nobility had embraced Protestantism and at the end of James' reign he was said to be in possession of a blacklist of 350 noblemen against whom he could institute proceedings for heresy, should he choose to do so.

That said, it would appear that Robert Lauder of Bass was not one of them. In 1542 he completed restoration work on St.Baldred's Chapel on The Bass (the previous restoration of this church had been in 1493), and in the same year his son, the already-mentioned John Lauder, Archdeacon of Tweedddale, represented Cardinal David Beaton at its reconsecration as a Roman Catholic chapel.

The Queen bore James V two boys in successive years, 1540 & 1541, named James and Arthur. However, the King's health had not been good and disaster was not far off. In April, 1541 both of the King's sons died suddenly and such was his grief that the Queen felt obliged to overcome her own to comfort him. At the same time conspiracies were rife in Europe, with new treaties and counter-alliances being entered into by almost everyone. Inevitably, Henry VIII expected

112

James would be dragged into this mess on the side of France, against whom Henry was busy preparing for war. This was, in fact, an error.

Henry resolved to invade Scotland. Francis I sent word to Scotland that France could not assist, yet it was as the ally of both France and the Papacy that James faced the impending invasion, and neither the *auld alliance* nor the Catholic Church commanded universal loyalty. Flodden was still deeply ingrained in people's memories and to add to the depressing scene was the King's personal unpopularity.

The army of 30,000 men which the King mustered on the Burgh Muir of Edinburgh in the autumn in no way resembled the enthusiastic host which had followed James IV to Flodden. The mood of the commanders was dangerously akin to those who had accompanied James III to Lauder.

In August 1542 Sir Robert Bowes had mounted a raid into Tweeddale which came to grief at Hadden Rig near Berwick, where he was routed by a Scottish force under the Earl of Huntly. However the English had taken and held several castles and tower-houses. On the 15th August 1542 King James V sent an order to the Captain of Dunbar Castle to blow up the Lauder's Edrington Castle "with two half-barrels of powder" (seems scarcely sufficient) because it had been taken and stengthened by the English. The Captain was told to consult William Lauder "the man of most experience within the said castle". However it is clear this order was never carried out.[61]

Henry VIII, still fuming after James V had failed to turn up at a meeting in York, as agreed, despatched the Duke of Norfolk to the north with an invasion army. James marched to Fala Muir, a plateau near the western end of the Lammermuir Hills. Norfolk had had difficulties with mutinous troops and after a looting, spoiling and burning exercise in the Borders, retreated to his own side of the

---

[61] This is almost certainly Robert Lauder of The Bass's illegitimate son, the elder William. This Order is printed in *The Melvilles, Earls of Melville, and the Leslies, Earls of Leven,* by Sir William Fraser, KCB., LL.D., Edinburgh, 1890, vol.ii, Correspondence, p.2.

Border. James realising the Scots unexpected advantage, wished to pursue him and bring him to battle.

But his orders to advance into England brought him face to face with the failure of his relations with the nobility. The commanders refused to obey the King and there was talk of a repetition of the Lauder Bridge hangings. However, it came to nothing. The army, however, disbanded, and the utterly humiliated King rode back to Edinburgh.
James was still resolved upon military action against England, in which he was still convinced that the Scots possessed the advantage. His half-brother Moray and Cardinal Beaton now raised an army which marched to Haddington where they encamped.

The King, with Lord Maxwell, Warden of the Western Marches, then gathered a further 10,000 men under 'privy letters' rather than a national muster, and marched to the west, to Lochmaben, where James suddenly became ill and was confined in the Castle.

Insisting that the invasion continue without him the army marched south during the night of the 24th November, and in the morning encountered and English force under Sir Thomas Wharton, the Governor of Carlisle, near the Solway Moss - a marshy area beside the River Esk. The result was the total rout of the Scots by an English force which numbered no more than 1,200 men. Fortunately there were few Scottish casualties, but the number of prisoners equalled that of the English soldiers! Cardinal Beaton disbanded his Haddington force and returned to Edinburgh.

James seemed to give way to despair. Regardless of the fact that he was now obviously quite seriously ill he rode aimlessly from place to place. Wandering from Tantallon Castle to Edinburgh, he then called at Linlithgow where Queen Marie was in the last month of her third pregnancy, and then proceeded through Fife and on to Falkland. On the 8th December Marie de Guise bore the daughter who was to become Mary Queen of Scots. James V, still at Falkland, died on the 14th. The Earl of Arran was now elected Governor, and the *General*

Index to the Acts of the Parliaments of Scotland tells us that one of those who voted for him was Henry Lauder, Lord St.Germains.

Henry VIII moved quickly and by August 1543 Arran had negotiated, in the Treaty of Greenwich, the betrothal of Mary, Queen of Scots, to the King's six-year-old son, the Prince of Wales. Another important product of this treaty, often overlooked, was the Scots agreement to authorise the Latin bible to be available in the Scottish vernacular. This was to have a profound effect upon Scottish history.

The Earl of Angus now returned to Scotland along with the nobles captured at Solway Moss, who included the Earls of Cassillis and Glencairn, and the Lords Maxwell, Fleming, Somerville and Gray. All had become pensioners of England and had pledged to support the English interest and to further the projected marriage. Thenceforward they were referred to in Scotland as the 'English Lords'.

The Scots soon repudiated the marriage contract. An angry Henry once more ordered the invasion of Scotland and instructed Edward Seymour, 8th Earl of Hertford, "to turn upside down the Cardinal's [Beaton] town of St Andrews....... sparing no creature alive within the same". Hertford led two invasions, in 1544 and 1545, and whilst he did not reach St.Andrews, he did untold destruction in southern Scotland, to buildings, to the population, to farms and livestock.

Crossing the Tweed he "birnd and destrued the nonery cald Coldstreme, so to Fogga [Fogo] and thair campeit that nyght, and many a town [farmstead] birnd that day, and a Monday Downes [Duns] tower and towne awaretrown [overthrown] and birnd all the pares which is L. [the parish which has fifty] towns and villages belonging to the said Downes; and the next day to West Nysbed [Nisbet] which was birnd and owairtrown tha castell, and many mor."[1] There is added a list of fifty two places burnt in the parish and "the Tower of Dunce raced [razed]." Bunkle Castle was also destroyed in Hertford's raid of 1544, together with the towers of Blanerne and

---

[1] *Proceedings* of the Society of Antiquaries of Scotland 1851-4. pp 275, 278.

Billie. Edinburgh and the Palace and Abbey of Holyrood were burnt, and the famous border abbeys reduced to ruins.

The capital repaired itself, and Holyroodhouse was eventually rebuilt, but the ruins of the abbeys still bear witness today to this appallingly savage campaign. Finally, on the 27th February 1545, the Earl of Angus gained a measure of revenge at Ancrum Moor when he destroyed a raiding force led by Sir Ralph Evers and Sir Brian Latoun.

In May 1546 a group of conspirators which included Norman Leslie the son of the Earl of Rothes, and William Kirkaldy of Grange, the son of James Vl's Treasurer, gained access to Beaton's Castle of St.Andrews, murdered the Cardinal and appealed for English help. It is widely assumed that Henry VIII was behind the conspiracy. Arran laid siege to the castle but as his son was a hostage within he retreated and the castle eventually fell to a French expeditionary force. Fortunately for those rebels within the castle they were not condemned to death but sent, with their Chaplain, the famous John Knox, to man the galleys of the French navy.

Whilst Henry VIII died in January 1547, The Earl of Hertford, now Duke of Somerset, became Regent for the young King Edward VI, and retaliated to French intervention in Scotland with yet another invasion. On lst September an English army again crossed the border and nine days later it encountered a superior Scottish force of some 25,000 men under the Earl of Arran on the banks of the River Esk 7 miles east of Edinburgh near the farm of Pinkie, and St. Michael's Church.

The Duke of Somerset had with him 4000 cavalry, 80 cannon, and was supported offshore by an English fleet under Lord Clinton. Between the two armies was the river with the only bridge across strongly guarded by the Earl of Huntly. The English position was not at all good, especially when faced by a numerically superior force.

Somerset was, however, to be aided by the usual Scottish lack of strategy and communications between commanders plus the famous streak of anarchism that often prevailed within the ranks. On the 9th September the Scottish cavalry recklessly crossed to the English side of the river and proceeded to taunt the enemy to attack. The English heavy cavalry obliged, and in a brief but fierce action the Scots were destroyed as an effective fighting force. Counted amongst the dead was Sir Alexander Lauder of Haltoun, Knt.[62], husband of Janet, daughter of William 5th Lord Borthwick. His kinsman, Robert Lauder of The Bass survived to fight another day, and we shall hear more of him later.

Later that day Arran opened negotiations offering the English a safe conduct home and, if that were refused, the choice of personal combat between Somerset and Huntly, with each supported by twenty men. These overtures were rejected, and at 8 am on the 10th September the English moved forward to the assault. As he prepared to attack, Somerset witnessed the remarkable spectacle of the Scots abandoning their position and beginning to cross the river to the English side. Why they did so is still a mystery; it may have been through sheer impetuosity or as a realisation that the English were about to take St Michael's Hill.

Whatever their motives the Scots, once across the river, found themselves in a very dangerous position. Somerset was superior in cavalry and artillery and the open ground now occupied by the Scots was ideal for the application of both.

Argyll's Highlanders on the left of the Scottish line fled from the field after coming under fire from the English fleet, and the remains of the Scots cavalry on the right stood off from the battle. As a result both Scottish flanks were in the air.

Lord Grey's cavalry charged the Scots pikemen but could make little impression on the schiltron until the English artillery proceeded to rake the enemy formation. Pounded by cannon, handguns and

---

[62] National Records of Scotland RH6/1534.

archers, the schiltron disintegrated and the English cavalry seized its chance to deliver a charge which broke the Scots army. The pursuit became a massacre as nearly 10,000 of the Scots were cut down. The English loss was little more than 500. Somerset, however, failed to exploit his victory politically and by August 1548 Mary, Queen of Scots, was in France awaiting marriage with the Dauphin.

Chapter 8

CARBERRY HILL

Following Pinkie, Robert Lauder of Bass immediately retired firstly to his manor at Tyninghame where his wounds were treated by his already ill wife, Margaret, daughter of Sir Oliver Sinclair of Roslin and Pentland. In *The Grange of St. Giles* it is clearly stated that Sir Robert Lauder of The Bass was a "faithful adherent and supporter of Mary of Guise ... doing good service for her in Haddingtonshire against the English, and also upholding her authority in opposition to the Lords of the Congregation".

The Queen-Regent meanwhile seized the opportunity to appeal for French help to evict the English, embarking her daughter Mary to France as a bride for the Dauphin Francis, eldest son of Henry II and the utterly notorious Catherine de Medici. Some assistance was immediately sent as Sir James Balfour states in his *Annals* that in 1548 "Robert Lauder of Basse, with the French garisone of Dunbar castle, takes the Englisch provisione going from Berwick to Haddingtone; kills many shouldiors and takes the Governor of Haddingtone, named Wilford, prissoner". Wilford[63], who had been promised a peerage as Viscount Haddington, failed to recover from his wounds and died before he could be rewarded.

Haddington appears to have been a fortress of very great strength. Nothing gives us a more extraordinary view of its state than the account of the campaigns of 1548 and 1549, given by M. Beague, an officer who fought with the French auxiliaries sent to assist Mary de Guise. It is difficult to get a sight of the original, which seems to have been published in Paris in 1556. I will therefore quote from a translation. At the time, it was held by the English, and the combined Scottish and French armies were occupied in its beleaguerment for most of the campaign, a detailed account of which fills many pages of M. Beague's narrative. He then describes its condition:

---

[63] He was half-brother to Cecily Wilford, who married Edwin Sandys, Archbishop of York.

" The Fortress of *Haddingtoun* is quadrangular: 'Tis situated in the midst of a low plain, and is commanded by no Neighbouring Mountain nor Rising Ground:

'Tis environ'd with a large and Flat-bottom'd ditch, a strong *Curtain* of turf, a spacious Rampart and Good and Safe Breast-works: Four strong *Bastions* are conveniently plac'd at the four Corners of the Wall, and are in Lieu of so many *Plat-Forms* design'd to keep the weak Places from being Discover'd. Behind these, namely towards the most Champian Country, they had rais'd several Works of Earth, by way of *Plat-Forms* and *Ravelins*, where they planted a great many Guns of a middle Size, to Annoy us as we sat down befor the Place. Above these Fortification they had rear'd up a *Curtain* with *Fascines*, on which their Arquebusiers stood secure. Beihind and over against the Rampart of the first Wall, there is a deep Fossey, border'd with a strong *Curtain* and four *Turrets*, which fence and Enclose the *Donjeon*; and betwixt the Edge of the Fossey and the *Curtain* of this *Donjeon*, there are many Casmates close to, and level with the first Rampart, in which Arquebusiers may be plac'd for Guarding the second Fossey: So that, suppose the *Turrets*, which fence the wall of the *Donjeon*, should be ruined by the Cannon of the Besiegers, yet these *Casmates*, with the Help of such *Falsebrays* as are intermixed with them, would supply their Loss. The *Donjeon* itself cannot be batter'd but by one side, and that is guarded by the river of Tyn. Besides, they had rais'd a *Cavalier* on the most exposed place of its Rampart, and by this means had Shelter'd both the House and the Soldiers. In fine, the Fort is so very Convenient and Spacious, that the Garrison (in case of Necessity) may Retreat into it, draw up in order of Battle; Nay, and raise new Fortifications for a further defence. The *English* had Built it in the manner I have describ'd, probably because *Hadingtoun* is Situated in a fruitful and pleasant Country, nigh the Capital City, not very remote from the Centre of *Scotland*, and, for these reasons, fit to insult over and annoy the whole Kingdom; But I know not, if they considered that these otherways Great Conveniencies were attended with this notable Disadvantage, that the Place was not to be succour'd with Men nor Ammunition without a prevailing army. For, as I have said, it lyes almost in the Middle of *Scotland*, and at the distance of two Leagues from the Sea; and the *English* were not Master of such other places as were proper to cover and bring off those in *Hadingtoun*."

A military eye can easily discover that the place was well calculated for admitting of such defences as these being added to it, and that under their protection, in those days when the munitions of war were by no means what they are at present, they must have been pretty effective. The following curious anecdote is told by Beague, a few pages later:-

" By this means M. *de Desse* had an Opportunity of taking a narrow and leisurely Inspection of the Enemy's Works and Defences, and when Retiring he had the Pleasure to Witness a very notable and daring Attempt on one of those Highland Men that belong'd to the Earl of *Argile*. This fellow had by this time taken Notice of the *French* behaviour, and had seen them go Fearlessly forward upon the very Mouth of the Enemy's Cannon, which he being willing to imitate, went straight upon a Party of the *English*, that had engag'd a few *Frenchmen*, Commanded by Captain *Voquedemar,* and with incredditable Celerity Seizing one of them, in spite of Opposition truss'd him upon his Back, and in this Plight brough him to our Camp; where we observ'd that the Enrag'd Captive had Bit his Shoulder after so Butcherly a manner that he had almost Died of the Wound. M. *de Desse* rewarded the Action with a good Coat of Mail and

20 Crowns, a Compliment which the Highlander received with all imaginable Demonstration of Gratitude."

We shall content ourselves with one more extract from this most interesting book, which describes the night assault made by the French and Scottish forces, with the hope of carrying the town by *a coup de main*:-

"All Things 'being Prudently and Cautiously laid for the design'd Effort, about Eleven at Night, every one arm'd, the Heavens were o'er-spread with Darkness; yet M. *de Desse* was faithfully Conducted by a convenient and secret Avenue to the Gates of *Hadingtoun*, where he remain'd without being discover'd (such was our Silence and Diligence) till some of the Soldiers, after taking a Half-Moon before the Port, and killing three Centinels, made the walls resound with the Name of *France*; at the same time we attack'd the Enemy's Guard, and found that they did their Duty but negligently. By this time the Town was all in an Alarm: But our Men improv'd their time all they could in their respective Posts; some set upon those Granaries, which the *English* had plac'd at the Back of an adjacent Church; and others endeavour'd to break open the Port, and effect'd it so suddenly, that the Garrison had but little time to put themselves in a Posture of Defence. The Guard of *Italians* were all put to the Sword in a Minute, and the few *English*, who were upon Duty at some distance from the former, far'd no better; severals were killed in their Sleep; and those who awaken'd had but the Comfort to Die more feelingly. Thus, we had leisure enough not only to do great Execution, but also to have carry'd the Town with little or no Loss; but M. *de Desse* was wisely apprehensive lest some Ingenious Fallacy should lurk under a Fault so evidently palpable; he very well knew that *the most unusual Favours of Fortune are for the most part Hurtful and Fraudulent*: For these Reason he would not suffer his Men to run Head-long upon Success, but kept them altogether in one Body. The Enemy had but one Pass to defend, and therefore were not so much put to it as if they had been environ'd on all sides; and this Pass was very narrow, and was fenc'd with Trenches and other Earth-Works, from whence a few Men, by firing upon the Assailants, were able to defeat their Attempt. Yet, M. *de Desse* upon the Front of his Battalion, continued to gain Ground, and to give such Testimonies of Valour, that (if Fame proves not very Unjust) Posterity must needs know, that few of his Co-temporaries could come up to his Merit: He was nobly back'd by Men that had been taught to fear no Danger. Our Soldiers had already cry'd *Victory, Victory!* a Hundred times, and doubted not but She waited upon their Arms: For of 500 Men that oppos'd our Entry, some in their Shirts, with Swords and Daggers, others with Halberts, and most part without any arms at all, 250 lost their Lives upon the Spot; whilst, hitherto, not one Man had fallen on our side.

"Indeed, Fortune till this Minute had been so partial in our Favour, that we could not doubt of Victory; and nothing, but what happen'd, could have frustrat'd our Hopes. M. *de Desse* and his Men were expos'd to the Mouth of a double Cannon planted betwixt two Gabions, upon the narrowest place of that Avenue, which leads to the town; this Place we had not made ourselves Masters of as yet; and by chance it so fell out that a French Soldier, a Native of Paris (who not long before had been corrupted by the Enemy, and serv'd them as a Spy), was upon that very Spot of Ground: This Renegade, dreading the punishment he deserv'd, turn'd Desparate; and nak'd and unarm'd as he was, ran to the Cannon I have mention'd, and put fire to it; the Ball made its way thro' the close Ranks of our Men, and could not miss of making a great Slaughter among them. For this Reason and because of the Obscurity of the Night, which kept us from the knowledge of the real Loss we had sustain'd (which yet was not such as to have depriv'd us of Success), behold a terrible Cry that seem'd to be made up of several voices, join'd as 'twere in one, was raised all over our Battalion,:

And *as the least Accident is sufficient to defeat the best laid of Nocturnal Attempts, by reason of the false Imaginations that ever attended them,* these confus'd Voices no sooner reach'd our Rear, than those who were upon it began to retire; their neighbours did the like by Degrees, and at last all broke their Ranks in Confusion and Disorder.

M. *de Desse*, with a good Number of the most Resolute at his Back, stood his Ground; and, still aiming at Victory, he could not forbear to evidence how much he grudg'd the lost Opportunity: Yet, at last, upon the Remonstrances of his Friends, who told him that evident Death was by no means to be sought for, and that Fortune might afterwards atone for her present Injustice, he gave Orders to sound a Retrait; and accordingly drew back with that Decency which the Occasion requir'd. Thus, with the Loss of some of his Men, and much the greater Slaughter of the Enemy, he got clear of further Danger: and prudently dissembling his Thoughts upon the Matter, he smil'd and said to the Lord *d' Oisel, 'Let us then suppose, my Friend, that we are at Sea, and by Storm constrain'd to lower our Sails, what then? The wind is changeable, and a fairer Gale will yet enable us to make out the Voyage.'"*

By this time The Bass had become an important fortress and in Mr Rapin's *History* it is listed, with Edinburgh, Dunotyre & Stirling, as one of "the principal castles in Scotland". During 1548-49 the English tried to secure The Bass, both by force and bribery, but both failed. M Beague also gives a description of it, and in particular of the hazards of landing upon it. He notes that the garrison numbered 120.

Marie de Guise retained the Earl of Arran's governorship of Scotland and to reward his compliance and encourage his further support he received the French title of Duke of Chatelherault. His half-brother, the erstwhile Abbot of Paisley, lately the Bishop of Dunkeld, was advanced to the Archbishopric of St.Andrews. By 1554 Marie had such a firm following that she was able to persuade Chatelherault to resign his governorship. French influence was once again dominant in Scotland, which would again, as in the past, be manipulated in the interests of France.

In 1553 the Protestant Edward VI of England died, to be succeeded briefly by the equally reformed Lady Jane Grey, his cousin, who in turn was hurriedly executed by Edward's Catholic half-sister Mary Tudor, who achieved notoriety for her actions against reformers and earned herself the nickname 'Bloody Mary'. She married Philip II of Spain. France and Spain were at war and by 1557 it appeared that France would be calling upon Scotland to assist her by attacking England once more. At that time Calais was the last remnant of England's medieval empire in France and the French were proposing to take it. They urged the Scots to attack Berwick-upon-Tweed, a town and castle they assumed the Scots would be eager to recover.

The Scottish nobility, however, knew that Berwick was forewarned and more than ready, and were tiring of the *Auld Alliance*. They were also restless at the continuing presence of the French garrisons in Scottish fortresses. In January 1558 Calais fell to the French without the Scots having moved against Berwick. A few months later, Queen Mary Tudor died.

Yet because of the internal strife and rival political and religious factions Scotland was too weak to stand alone. The attempts of Henry VIII and Somerset to impose English domination had been frustrated, but only at the cost of permitting a form of French domination which was beginning to appear, to some, scarcely more palatable.

On the 24th April 1558, Mary, Queen of Scots, was married to the Dauphin Francis in the Cathedral of Notre-Dame in Paris. They assumed the titles of 'King and Queen of Scots, Dauphin and Dauphiness of France'. However, in secret documents signed three weeks before the marriage, Mary bequeathed her Kingdom to the Royal House of France (Valois) in the event of her death without issue. It was also without the enthusiasm of his Scottish subjects that Francis was granted the *Crown Matrimonial,* which gave him the right to reign in Scotland should his wife predecease him. Mary, by her descent from Margaret Tudor, also laid claim to England.

However, other forces were also now at work in Scotland. Lutheranism had been overtaken by the stronger influence of Calvinism, which gained a tenacious hold upon the country during the 1550s and 1560s. And, the new English monarch, Elizabeth, daughter of Henry VIII and Ann Bullen (or Boleyn), was a confirmed Protestant.

The Reformation in Scotland moved fast and some members of the nobility, with their eyes on the vast wealth of the Church, had organised themselves, under the leadership of Lord James Stewart, into the 'Lords of the Congregation of Christ Jesus' (the Confederate Lords) and took a Covenant to drive out the Regent and her French adherents and correct the "hated errors" of the Roman faith. In May 1559 John Knox returned from exile and his inflammatory preaching incited the people. The multitude rose. At Perth, Scone, Stirling, St.Andrews and Edinburgh churches and Abbeys succumbed to the mob in assaults of militant Calvinism.

On the 6th July Henri II of France was accidentally killed at a tournament. Francis and Mary would now assert their rights. The Confederate Lords, desperate, appealed for *English* assistance to resist Mary and the French and in October formally declared the Regency of

126

Marie de Guise at an end. Mary fortified herself in Leith and appealed for further reinforcements from France.

Meanwhile, Queen Elizabeth signed the Treaty of Berwick with the Confederate Lords in February 1560, and this therefore gave her the excuse to intervene against the French, and Catholicism, and to secure Scotland, at last, as England's ally. Arguing that the treaty was one of mutual defence and that Scotland was threatened by France, the English army and fleet arrived in March to besiege the fortress of Leith, receiving, amazingly, a great welcome in Scotland. However, Marie de Guise was terminally ill and died on the 11th June. By the Treaty of Edinburgh signed the following month the French agreed to evacuate Scotland.

John Knox arguing with Mary, Queen of Scots

The Parliament which met in August 1560 was a crowded session attended by many minor barons, amongst them those of Lauder of The Bass, and Sir William Lauder of Haltoun. This first Reformation Parliament was to split the ancient family of Lauder, and also the nation. The Lauders had provided many sons of the Church over the centuries and Robert of The Bass (d.1576) had remained firm in his defence of the 'true faith'. Two of his sons were priests and two of his wife's brothers were Bishops. This Parliament adopted a Calvinist *Confession of Faith* as the definition of the new State Religion and prohibited the celebration of Mass. This was also a bad year for the French all round, as Francis II also died. Mary was no longer Queen of France.

Mary, Queen of Scots, returned to Scotland in the summer of 1561. Her great undoing, in the forthcoming years, was her desire to also succeed to the Crown of England. She sent her secretary William Maitland of Lethington (whose sister Mary married Sir Alexander Lauder of Haltoun, d.1627) to London to press her claim. He was sent packing by Elizabeth. Mary decided to force Elizabeth's hand by marrying 'powerfully'. She announced that she would marry her cousin, Henry Stewart, Earl of Darnley, grandson of the Earl of Angus - Margaret Tudor's second husband. He had, therefore, a claim in his own right to the English and Scottish thrones and his marriage to Mary united the two branches of the descendants of Margaret. Darnley was also a devout Roman Catholic. Elizabeth protested, and the Scottish Protestants organised a rebellion under the Earl of Sutherland, but they were defeated by Lord James Stewart, whom Mary had recently elevated to the Earldom of Moray, at the Battle of Corrichie on 28th October 1562. The rebel Earl of Huntly himself collapsed and died, apparently of a stroke, immediately after the battle and one of his sons was executed.

However, the usual ever-moving allegiances of the higher Scottish nobility saw many changing sides for both religious and political reasons. Thus the Earls of Moray, Chatelherault, Argyll and Glencairn[64] rose again following Mary's marriage in 1565 but were driven, by Mary herself at the head of her army, across the Border into England. Mary became over-confident. To Philip of Spain and the Pope she applied for assistance for a (Roman Catholic) religious crusade, and confiscated the lands of those who had been involved in the recent risings.

Darnley's shortcomings soon became apparent and Mary turned for political advice to an Italian, David Riccio, who had arrived in Scotland in 1561 in the household of the ambassador of Savoy. She made Riccio her secretary in charge of her French correspondence. A group of Lords who had sympathised with Moray, although not participated in his rebellion, plotted the death of "the detested papist foreigner" whose rise and influence they resented. Amongst these plotters was Sir William Lauder of Haltoun,[1] the Earl of Morton, and Lords Lindsay and Ruthven. Morton was Darnley's nephew.

Darnley, who had been inflamed to "murderous jealousy" joined the conspirators. In March 1566, the Queen was six months pregnant and Darnley believed that the child was Riccio's. On the evening of the 9th the Queen and the Countess of Argyll, her half-sister, were at supper in a little room off the bedchamber in Holyrood House. Riccio was in attendance. Suddenly, Darnley unexpectedly joined them. Lord Ruthven then appeared, clad in armour, followed by the rest of the conspirators who seized Riccio who was clinging, shrieking, to the Queen's skirts.

Mary was restrained by Darnley and Riccio was dragged from the room and stabbed with many weapons, which the murderers left stuck in the corpse.

---

[64] Glencairn's daughter, Susanna, married Alexander Lauder, younger of Haltoun, *d.v.p., s.p.* 1623.

[1] It is clear that Sir William continued to pop up in dangerous places, as on the 13th June 1593, just three years before his death, an entry in the *Register of the Privy Council of Scotland* notes that he was wounded in the head, and Mr James Bishop slaughtered, by the Provost and Baillies of Edinburgh while the latter were arresting one Thomas Henderson.

On 17th March 1566, Sir Robert Lauder of Popill, Knt., younger of The Bass, was appointed Captain of Tantallan Castle, the Keeper being the Earl of Atholl.[65] This appointment followed the surrender of Sir William Douglas of Lochleven who was one of those charged wih the murder of Rizzio.[66]

The assassination of Rizzio, Mary Queen of Scots secretary. Sir William Lauder of Haltoun was one of the conspirators.

The Queen was now threatened by Moray and his associates who returned from England to Edinburgh and forced her to pardon them. With Darnley in tow, she escaped to take refuge in the Earl of Bothwell's castle at Dunbar. Morton, Lindsay and Ruthven now fled to England. Reinforced, Mary accompanied by the Earls of Atholl, Huntly and others, returned in triumph to Edinburgh. Darnley had

---

[65] *Accounts of the Lord High Treasurer of Scotland,* vol.XI, 1559 - 1566, Edinburgh 1916, p: lxxi.
[66] Young, M.A., Margaret D., editor, *The Parliaments of Scotland - Burgh & Shire Commissioners* vol.2, Edinburgh, 1993, p.407.

betrayed firstly Mary and then his conspiratorial comrades. None were disposed to forgive or forget.

The future King James VI of Scotland was born on the 19th June, 1566. The Queen announced to Darnley, in the presence of Sir William Stanley, that "God has given you and me a son, begotten by none but you!".

At Craigmillar Castle[67] in November, a conference between the Queen, the Earls of Moray, Bothwell, Huntly and Argyll, and William Maitland of Lethington, took place to decide how to dispense with Darnley. On Christmas Eve Mary pardoned the murderers of Riccio and those who remained in England returned in January. The Queen had now become infatuated with Bothwell into whose hands the latest conspiracy was placed. Although Morton declined involvement in yet another murder, matters nevertheless progressed. In February the Queen installed Darnley, who was ill at the time, in a house on the outskirts of Edinburgh called *Kirk o' Field*. On the night of the 9th January 1567, the house was utterly destroyed by a huge explosion. However, Darnley's body was later found in the garden. He had been strangled. Darnley's father, the Earl of Lennox brought the Earl of Bothwell to trial, but as the courtroom was packed by Mary and Bothwell with their supporters, he was "acquitted for want of evidence".

There was now an outcry against Bothwell. Notwithstanding this, and heeding not a cautionary letter from Elizabeth, Mary married Bothwell on the 15th May 1567. To make matters worse, Bothwell had only just completed a hasty divorce from Lady Jean Gordon whom he had married only the year before! Although Bothwell was a great Border magnate, with castles at Bothwell, Crichton, Hailes, Hermitage and Dunbar, he had no network of alliances, and many enemies. Because of her behaviour, both moral and political, Mary had forfeited the

---

[67] Elizabeth, daughter of Robert Lauder of The Bass and his second wife, Lady Elizabeth Hay of the Yester family, would marry David Preston, Lord of Craigmillar, in 1575.

support of much of her nobility and her marriage to Bothwell left them both isolated and vulnerable.

The Confederate Lords decided upon a showdown and led by the Earl of Morton assembled their army at Edinburgh. Mary was still Queen, however, and many felt they were absolutely bound by their oaths of allegiance. One of these was Robert Lauder of The Bass (d.1576).[68] He was one of the many Lowland Barons who joined the Queen's army which departed Dunbar on the 14th June 1567, and advanced to Seaton. Her next step was to entrench herself on Carberry Hill within the old works which had been thrown up by the English army prior to the Battle of Pinkie.

Holinshed's *Chronicle* tells us "There were with the Queen and Bothwell, the Lords Seiton, Yester, and Bothwike, also the *lairds* of Waughton, Bass, Ormiston, Weaderburne, Blackater and Langton. They had with them also two hundred harquebusiers waged, and of great artillerie some field peeces. Their whole number was esteemed to be about 2000." It is worth adding here that Sir Robert Lauder of Bass had a vested interest in Queen Mary as in 1566 he had lent her and Darnley £2000, a huge sum at the time.[69]

On the 15th June 1567, Mary's opponents marched from Edinburgh, their arrival on the scene of the impending conflict creating a general panic in the Queen's army, desertion being so rapid that she and Bothwell were left with only sixty gentlemen and a band of hack-butters. Bothwell then wished to decide the issue by single combat and sent Morton a challenge, but Morton declined and at the Queen's insistence Bothwell escaped on horseback from the field. He eventually reached Denmark where his past caught up with him and he was imprisoned. He died in captivity in 1578. Mary never saw him again after Carberry Hill.

---

[68] Young, 1884, p.52.
[69] *The Register of The Privy Council of Scotland* vol.iii, Edinburgh 1880, p.118/119.

The Queen surrendered to her enemies and was conducted back to the capitol riding between the Earls of Morton and Atholl. The populace crowded around them screaming "burn the whore!" She was imprisoned in the island fortress of Lochleven castle, her gaoler being Moray's half-brother. On the 24th July she abdicated and the Earl of Moray became Regent for the 13 month old James VI, who although baptised as a Catholic, was crowned as a Protestant Monarch.

The Battle of Reidsweir

On the 2nd May 1568, Mary escaped, and taking advantage of the usual discord between the power-hungry nobles, rallied nine Earls, eighteen Lords, nine Bishops and twelve commendators to her cause. Of the nobles in her force was the fiercely loyal Robert Lauder of The Bass and his son & heir-apparent, Sir Robert Lauder of Popill, Knt., John, Patrick and Charles, brothers of Robert jnr.[70] Their combined

---

[70] Donaldson, D.Litt., Gordon, editor, *Register of the Privy Seal of Scotland 1567 – 1574*, vol.6, Edinburgh, 1963, numbers 502 & 503, p.102, where all the Lauders were escheated for taking part in this battle. This escheat was later lifted.

followings raised an estimated 6000 men. However, this second Royal army was defeated by Moray on the 13th May at Langside, near Glasgow. Mary fled on the 16th May to England where she was imprisoned. Yet she continued to be involved in a variety of conspiracies, the last being one with Anthony Babington, a young Roman Catholic courtier, to assassinate Elizabeth of England. Finally, on the 8th February 1587, Mary Stewart, Queen of Scots, was beheaded for treason at Fotheringay Castle.

Not long before this execution, in 1575, the last battle between the Kingdoms of England and Scotland took place at Carter Bar, anciently called Reidswire, 1,370 feet above sea level, on the Border. It was the custom in the Middle Ages for the Wardens of the Marches on both sides of the Border to meet periodically to settle disputes and punish those who had committed crimes on both sides. In 1575 such a meeting took place between Sir J Carmichael, the Keeper of Liddesdale, and Sir John Forster, the English Warden (the Forster family seat for centuries was Bamburgh Castle).

For a while the business of the day was conducted peaceably. Then a dispute arose over the famous English freebooter, the oddly-named Farnstein. High words passed until the Tynedale men started the battle with a flight of arrows. The famous ballad *The Raid of the Reldswire* tells the story:

Yett was our meeting meek eneugh
Begun wi' merriment and mowes,
And at the brae aboon the heugh
The clark sat down to call the rowes [Rolls],
And some for kyne and some for ewes
Call'd in of Dandrie, Hob and Jock -
We saw come marching ower the knowes
Five hundred Fenwicks in a flock.

With jack and speir and bows all bent,
and warlike weapons at their will;

134

Although we were na well content,
Yet, by my troth, we fear'd no ill.
Some gaed to drink, and some stude still,
And some to cards and dice them sped;
Till on ane Farnstein they fyled a bill,
And he was fugitive and fled.

Carmichael bade them to speak out plainlie
And cloke no cause for ill or good;
The other answering him as vainlie
Began to reckon kin and blood
He raise and raxed [stretched] him where he stood
And bade him match him with his marrows;
Then Tindaill heard them reason rude,
And they loos off a flight of arrows.

In the ensuing skirmish the Scots were victorious, the English retreating for three miles leaving many dead and prisoners. However, a few weeks later the prisoners were released by the Scots to prevent a war developing between the two kingdoms.

Chapter 9

JAMES VI

King James VI had, as his guardians, the Earls of Mar, and Morton (a Douglas), with the Earl of Moray as Regent.

Moray proved himself a capable ruler, imposing some significant degree of civil order and suppressing general lawlessness. Many ordinary people thought him the best ruler of Scotland for years. However, the Hamilton Duke of Chatelherault was aggrieved that Moray was Regent, and not himself as had been the case during Mary's minority. Moray's principal weakness therefore lay in his failure either to defeat the Hamiltons decisively or win their support. Their castles, the centres of their strength, remained in their hands despite their defeat at Langside.

On the 23rd January 1570, Regent Moray was shot dead from the 'forstair' of a house as he rode through the town of Linlithgow, by James Hamilton of Bothwellhaugh. The house was owned by Chatelheralt's half-brother, Archbishop Hamilton of St Andrews, a resolute opponent of the new regime. The horse that Bothwellhaugh escaped upon was lent to him by Lord John Hamilton, the Duke's son.

Moray's death was a severe blow to the King's party. Stupidly, the Hamiltons and some others now launched a border raid into England. This provided the pretext for a small-scale English invasion who joined forces with the King's party and finally destroyed the palace, castle and town of Hamilton. With Elizabeth's approval, the King's paternal grandfather, the Earl of Lennox, became the new Regent and his prestige was greatly enhanced when, in 1571, he took the castles of Doune and Dumbarton which had remained in the hands of the Queen's party. In the latter castle, Archbishop Hamilton was taken prisoner and on the 7th April he was hanged in Stirling. (Until his death c.1555, John Lauder, the 'Public Accuser' and Archdeacon of Teviotdale, had been Hamilton's Secretary following Beaton's murder).

What part Sir Thomas Ker, the Laird of Fairnyhurst Castle, near Jedburgh, played in the disruption of the time is not clear, but he was busy with a number of followers raiding Liddisdale, Eskdale, Annandale etc., and on the 12th February 1571 a Bond for their pursuit was subscribed at Jedburgh by numerous knights and lairds, one of whom was Gilbert Lauder of Whitslaid, near Lauder, brother-in-law to the Laird of Haltoun.

The last bastion of Mary's supporters were fortified in Edinburgh Castle under the joint command of Kirkaldy of Grange and William Maitland of Lethington. (The connexion between the various Lords is demonstrated on 13th September this year when Sir "Robert Lauder of Popill, knycht" was called upon to pay a debt to the receiver for the confiscated estates of "William Maitland, sumtyme apperand of Lethingtoun" represented by Captain David Hume.[71] Exempted along with his father, Robert Lauder of The Bass, from military service being "hevelie vexit with infirmitie of the gravell" (kidney stones) 1569-1572, they escaped this conflict.. Although Sir Robert was formerly a Marian, he now became a supporter of the Regent Morton and the King's party in 1572. [72]

Grange & Lethington were joined for a time by Chatelherault and his other son Lord Claud Hamilton. Morton based himself at Leith and in the summer of 1571 began to lay siege to the castle. In the meantime most of the citizens left as the city precincts became a battlefield. Lennox had secured the loyalty of the Earls Eglinton, Cassillis and Argyll and a number of other nobles who had previously adhered to the Queen. In August, it was decided to hold a Parliament at Stirling. Morton duly departed Leith for the meeting and there was a temporary lull in the fighting.

Grange decided to take advantage of Stirling's vulnerability and planned a night attack, hoping to catch the nobles therein by surprise.

[71] *Registers of the Privy Council*, vol.ii, Edinburgh, 1878, pps.80/81.
[72] Young, M.D., 1993, vol.ii, Edinburgh, 1993, p.407-8.

The attack was led by the Earl of Huntly and Lord Claud Hamilton, who speedily forgot Grange's orders to bring back the prisoners in safety so that they could be used as bargaining pawns. A messy attack ensued, with much street-fighting and looting. The Earl of Mar led a sally from the castle, the raiders were repulsed and most of the prisoners rescued. The Regent, however, was shot in the back and died of his wounds. The little King, now five, saw his grandfather carried mortally wounded into Stirling Castle in the early morning.

The Parliament met and elected the Earl of Mar, a highly respected man of great integrity, as the new Regent. In Edinburgh, Grange bitterly abused Huntly and Lord Claud Hamilton as 'disorderly beasts'. He realised the new gravity of their position. The bitter civil war continued in Edinburgh during the winter, and the spring of 1572.

During the summer a truce was arranged and Chatelherault, Lord Claude Hamilton, Huntly and Lord Seton took the opportunity to leave the castle, leaving Grange to his own devices. Lethington was slowly dying of a paralytic disease.

Unexpectedly, the Earl of Mar suddenly died and was succeeded by the last of the Regents elected to rule on behalf of James VI - the Earl of Morton. Archbishop Mathew called this Regency - 'the last great showing of the Douglas blood'. James Douglas, 4th Earl of Morton, was born about 1516 the son of Sir George Douglas the younger brother of the Earl of Angus. When the family were banished by James V, the young James Douglas fled north and worked as on overseer in the Highlands. He married Lady Elizabeth Douglas daughter of the 3rd Earl of Morton, and succeeded to his father-in-law's title in right of his wife.

Morton was formally installed as Regent on the 21st November 1572, the day of John Knox's death. Tiring of the situation in Edinburgh, he negotiated for English help in reducing the Castle at the beginning of May 1573. Elizabeth sent a force under Sir William Drury, of the famous Suffolk family, also Marshal of Berwick-upon-Tweed, with

'20 grate pieces' of ordnance to batter down the defences. Grange surrendered on the 29th May. Lethington later died in Leith Prison.

The Regent was, as James VI would be after him, beset by enormous financial burdens and severe economic problems. He was, for instance, unable to halt the chronic depreciation of the Scottish pound. Before long, the familiar patter of events took over. A good example of the closing of ranks in the various camps was the "Band of Roxburgh" in 1576, where many of the aristocracy, including Sir William Lauder of Haltoun, swore allegiance to the Earl of Morton. The first plot against Morton occurred in 1578 shortly before James's twelfth birthday, and was a consequence of a feud between the Earls of Athol and Argyll. They had been disciplined by Morton, in Council, and as a result promptly laid aside their differences and made common cause against the Regent.

Athol and Argyll involved the young King who was, of course, greatly flattered by their requests, and he asked for Morton's resignation which was immediately given. On the 12th March, 1578, the King's *acceptance of the government* was proclaimed in Edinburgh. The next nine years witnessed a series of coups d'etat, from which the King was to emerge somewhat disillusioned.

In the autumn of 1579 Lord Esme Stuart d'Aubigny arrived from his estate in France to secure his position in the line of succession and his rights to the Lennox title. The King became infatuated with this gentleman and before the end of the year had bestowed upon him the Abbey of Arbroath, one of the forfeited properties of the Hamiltons, and early the following year James persuaded Lord Robert Stuart to resign his recently granted title of Earl of Lennox to d'Aubigny.

Plot number two against the unfortunate Morton now took shape. The new Earl of Lennox persuaded Captain James Stewart, younger son of Lord Ochiltree, to accuse Morton of being involved in Darnley's murder, some thirteen years after the event! On the 31st December 1580 Morton was imprisoned and on the 2nd June 1581 he was publicly executed in Edinburgh by guillotine, which, ironically, Morton himself introduced into Scotland.

Having assured the naive young King that Morton was really his enemy the King was duly pleased at this latest exercise in travesties of justice and Esme Stuart was rewarded with the Dukedom of Lennox and James Stewart was created Earl of Arran (even though the current Earl, who had been declared insane, did not die until 1609!).

John Knox had been the acknowledged leader of the Kirk. Following his death he was replaced in 1574 when the reformer Andrew Melville returned to Scotland from Geneva and he began a new and more vigorous phase of the Kirk's war against episcopacy. This clarion call found brother turning upon brother and suspicion was rife, akin to the inquisition. The Dean of Restalrig, James Lauder, 3rd but eldest surviving son and heir-apparent of Robert Lauder of The Bass (d.1576) was murdered by his 1st cousin, Walter Lauder, in October 1580 in Beil Tower, East Lothian. Pitcairn's *Criminal Trials* gives us the details and records that the trial took place on the 15th December, 1580. Walter was found guilty and beheaded.

Lennox, despite his hasty conversion to Protestantism, was regarded as a Catholic agent sufficient to cause a kind of anti-Catholic hysteria in the Kirk. In 1581 William Ruthven, 1st Earl of Gowrie and an extreme Protestant, detained the King at Ruthven Castle and ordered Lennox to leave Scotland immediately, which he did, dying in France two years later. This act was to leave an indelible blot upon the King's mind in all his future dealings with the Kirk.

James escaped, with two companions, one of whom was Sir James Melville, to St.Andrews where he was joined by the Earls of Montrose, Rothes, Argyll, Huntly, and Crawford and by the recently created Earl of Arran. Sir James Melville described Arran as 'a scorner of all religion, presumptuous, covetous, a despiser of the nobility and of all honest men'.

It is recorded that in 1581 the new feudal baron of The Bass, George Lauder (4th but now eldest surviving son of Robert Lauder of The Bass), granted King James VI and his suite temporary accommodation in his castle on the gaunt isle. The King was so enamoured that he offered to buy the island, a proposition which did not commend itself to George Lauder. The King appears to have accepted the situation with good grace. George had been a priest and an advocate and a Privy Counsillor - described as the King's "familiar councillor" – and was later tutor to the young Prince Henry.[73] It may be that after the affair at Ruthven Castle James was feeling somewhat insecure, regardless of his supporters, and saw in the *laird* of The Bass a traditionally loyal supporter with a fortress that was utterly impregnable which he could retire to in some safety.

The Earl of Gowrie was executed in 1584. His allies, the young Earl of Mar, Morton's nephew Angus, the Earl of Glencairn, the Master of Glamis and Francis Stewart Earl of Bothwell (nephew of Mary's husband) had fled to England. In the autumn of 1585, with a measure of English support, they returned to Scotland, appearing before Stirling in force, on the 2nd November. Arran was driven from Court, and deprived of his Earldom. He was finally murdered in 1595 by James Douglas of Parkhead, a nephew of Morton.

In 1586, John Maitland of Thirlestane (the younger brother of William of Lethington), a lawyer, in his new role as Secretary of Scotland and *Keeper of the Great Seal,* negotiated a formal League with England. This was also the year in which John Maitland purchased the old former Crown Fort, on the Leader Water below Lauder, and began his plans for the new Thirlestane Castle on the site. Furthermore, on the 20th August 1589 King James VI married Princess Anne of Denmark, a Lutheran.

On the 17th May 1590, "the queene" was crowned in the Abbey Kirk, Edinburgh. Before she went out of her chamber, the Chancellor was

---

[73]"The Bass Rock in History" in *Transactions of the East Lothian Antiquarian and Field Naturalists' Society*, Fifth volume, 1948, p.55.

made a Lord of Parliament as Lord Thirlestane, and the *laird of Basse* (George Lauder) and several others were dubbed knights. "Maister George Lauder of Bass" is also included in a list dated 5th June 1592 of 'baronis, knichtis and gentlemen nominat to be of his hienes privie counsaill'. On the same day James VI also ratified "'ane act of secreit counsaill in favoris of the laird of the bass". In 1593 Sir George Lauder of Bass was appointed one of the commissioners to examine into James the Sixth's debts, and to make arrangements for his proposed visit to the Isles. Sir George, "his hienes Trustie and weil-belouit counsellour", was also, in October 1593, one of the "special persons" of the estates to whom was remitted the offers of the three Popish Lords, the Earls of Angus, Huntly, and Errol, to consider and determine. By 1598 Sir George was tutor to the young Prince Henry, elder brother of the future King Charles I. It is therefore quite clear where the Lauder family continued to place their loyalties, as the end of the sixteenth century drew to a close – firmly behind their legitimate sovereign, as had been the case since 1054. However, the cost had been great, especially in financial terms, and this would begin to show in the next century.

For complex reasons, but largely the usual ones of rivalry, some of the senior aristocracy continued to be a cause for concern, notably the Earl of Huntly and Francis Stewart, Earl of Bothwell. James VI decided to act. In the Autumn of 1594 the King mustered an army and marched into Aberdeenshire and a skirmish took place in Glenlivet between Huntly's forces and the advance guard of the King's army, led by the young Duke of Argyll. Huntly was forced to retreat to his castle of Strathbogie, which the King threatened to blow up unless Bothwell was handed over. Huntly let Bothwell escape and then himself retired abroad, followed in 1595 by Bothwell himself. The latter never returned, dying in Naples in 1612, but Huntly did, in 1596, and converted to Protestantism at the King's request.

Most of James' reign was spent in almost perpetual argument with the General Assembly of the Kirk over doctrine and episcopacy, with James receiving minor concessions on the latter. These differences seemed set to continue for the foreseeable future when, on the 24th

March 1603, Queen Elizabeth of England died. James VI of Scotland was proclaimed her successor as James 1st of England – the Union of the Crowns. James was 37 and had spent himself on his Herculean labours in Scotland. He ascended the throne in an ominous calm. England was not Scotland and the methods employed in the latter would not be appropriate in dealing with his new problems.

Chapter 10

END OF THE *ANCIEN REGIME*

James I & VI met his first English Parliament with no personal outstanding financial obligations but a massive national debt of £100,000 inherited from Elizabeth. The national debt in Scotland was more considerable; but the King's proposal for a legislative union between England & Scotland was rejected and relations with Parliament were not harmonious. In 1605 the Roman Catholic Guy Fawkes's attempt to blow up King, Lords and Commons caused a reconciliation. However, financial quarrels continued. James's view of the Royal prerogative also aroused opposition. Parliament was dissolved early in 1611 with the financial problems unsolved.

In 1613 James married his daughter Elizabeth to Frederick, Elector Palatine, a leading German Protestant. In 1618 Frederick was invited by the Protestants in Bohemia to accept its Crown, hitherto almost hereditary in the Roman Catholic Habsburg family. Frederick accepted, and the war which followed lasted for thirty years (1614-1648). James tried to mediate, without success. Protestants in Britain rallied to support the cause in Europe, the Parliament also expressing its support in 1621.

Then followed the somewhat ridiculous expedition of Prince Charles and the Duke of Buckingham to Madrid in an attempt to marry Charles to the King of Spain's daughter, and so seal an alliance by which James hoped to bring peace to Europe. This expedition was a humiliating failure. James died in February 1625, and his son, the new King Charles I, married Henrietta Maria, a Catholic Princess of France, an unpopular Union with both his Protestant people and Parliament.

George Lauder of The Bass, an only child who had succeeded his father, Sir George in 1611, spent considerable time, with his mother, at the Court of James 1st in London, but in March 1624 the Scottish Privy Coucil requested their return to Scotland and wrote accordingly to the King.[74] They were both back resident in their castle on The Bass in December 1628[75] and in 1634.[76]

Britain now became embroiled in the wars in both Spain and France. In the summer of 1627 The Duke of Buckingham decided to relieve the besieged La Rochelle and began an attempt to seize the island of Rhe, in its harbour. With him was Colonel George Lauder (1600-1670), the son of Sir Alexander Lauder of Haltoun, by his second wife Annabella Bellenden[77].[78] In 1622 after graduating from Edinburgh University George had joined the army, and 5 years later served at La Rochelle. He received his commission as captain in 1634 and became Lieut.-Colonel of Scott's regiment in 1657. He distinguished himself fighting against the Spanish at Callo; and at the Battle of Fune [Funen island], after which the King of Denmark presented him with a gold chain and his [the king's] portrait in diamonds [1659]. George was also a celebrated poet and correspondent. One of his poems, "Christian Meditations", was dedicated to "The Right Honourable my very loving [half] brother Richard Lauder, baron of Haltoun."[1661].

The battle for Rhe island had all the handicaps which normally paralysed Stuart expeditions and Buckingham, whilst himself showing courage and resources had to withdraw with heavy losses, and forty British flags were hung by the victorious French in Notre Dame. In August 1628 Buckingham was assassinated.

---

[74] Masson, David, LL.D., editor, *The Register of the Privy Council of Scotland*, Edinburgh, 1896, vol. xiii, 1622-1625, p.452/3.

[75] *Registrum Concilii Secreti*, 1628-9, fol.67, cited in Ritchie, 1880, pps: 56-8.

[76] Brown, P. Hume, MA., LL.D., editor, *The Register of the Privy Council of Scotland*, 2nd Series, volume v, Edinburgh, 1904, p.655.

[77] Daughter of Sir John Bellenden of Auchnoull & Broughton, Director of Chancery and Lord Justice-Clerk.

[78] It is stated in the 1908 *Dictionary of National Biography* that George was a grandson of Sir Richard Maitland of Lethington. However, this is an error as Sir Alexander Lauder's first wife, Mary Maitland, died some four years before George was born.

The English Parliament, which sat rarely, was formally dissolved on March 10th 1629 for their "undutitul and seditious carriage" and King Charles 1st began eleven years of personal rule. However a group of courtiers: Sir Richard Weston (a Catholic), and later Lord Cottington, and Henrietta Maria conspired until once again Catholicism became fashionable at Court, and in 1637 a Papal agent was received at Whitehall. Simultaneously several puritans were mutilated, heavily fined and imprisoned for life.

Richard Lauder

James had re-established Episcopacy in Scotland, despite the opposition. To make matters worse, the new King, spurred on by Archbishop Laud, tried to recover Church lands from the nobles who had seized them: somewhat dramatically, in 1625, Charles revoked all Royal and ecclesiastical lands alienated since 1542. Then, on the 18th

June 1633, Charles was belatedly crowned at Holyrood with the pomp and ceremony of the Church of England, as King of Scotland. In 1637 he introduced a slightly modified version of the English Prayer Book to replace Knox's Presbyterian *Book of Common Order*. Neither the Scottish Parliament nor the General Assembly of the Church of Scotland had been consulted and these actions touched off a Presbyterian national resistance movement. In 1638 the Presbyterian *National Covenant* was signed all over Scotland and those Scottish nobles who supported it duly mustered their feudal levies and their army moved towards the Border, commanded by a first-class soldier, Alexander Leslie, who had fought in the Swedish Armies under Gustavus Adolphus. Leslie was the illegitimate son of George Leslie of Balquhain, Captain of Blair Castle, and a "wench in Rannoch."

King Charles collected a small army to oppose the Scots, but he had no money to pay the reluctant troops. In June 1639 he had to sign the Treaty of Berwick after a bloodless campaign commonly called the First Bishop's War. But he refused to abolish Episcopacy in Scotland and negotiations were again broken off. Charles then recalled the English Parliament in April 1640 but they refused the King funds for his war with the Covenanters, and after three weeks Charles again dissolved Parliament. Seven traitorous English peers then made common cause with the rebel Scots and invited them into England.

In August the Covenanters' Army, estimated at 20,000 foot and 2,500 horse, crossed the Border and passed through Wooler, Eglingham and Netherwitton, Northumberland, bearing flags with the words *For Christ's Crown and Covenant*. Eventually they reached Newburn on the north side of the Tyne where the river was fordable at two places which were the nearest points to Newcastle. They encamped on Heddon-law above Newburn. The Royal Army, made up of a mere 3000 foot and 1,500 horse were drawn up on Stella Haugh, a meadow nearly one mile in length on the south of the river. At the two fords breastworks were built (traces of which were still visible less than 100 years ago).

148

The Scots, having the advantage of the higher ground above Newburn, overlooked all the Royalist troops. On the 28th August the Scots placed their cannon in Newburn village, even using the church steeple, with their foot hidden among the houses, lanes and hedges. The battle started with a Royalist musketeer hitting a Scottish trooper who was watering his horse in the Tyne. Leslie's troops replied with a heavy cannonade on the Royalist redoubts, which the latter soon abandoned, overcome by the general superiority of the Scots. A few hundred Scots cavalry and musketeers now crossed the river and before long the King's troops were in flight. The fight at Newburn hardly merits the title "battle". Clarendon, the historian of the Royalist side, described it as "that infamous, irreparable rout". The disaster at Newburn was, however, a major defeat for Charles. The Earl of Strafford, England's very competent Minister of War, evacuated Newcastle and the Covenanters entered the city the next day. Their victory had given them control of Northumberland and Durham.

The Covenanters marched on to Yorkshire where a peace treaty was signed at Ripon in October. A general British Civil War now appeared imminent with Charles 1st and his two Parliaments at almost complete loggerheads on a wide range of policies. Desultory negotiations took place as the forlorn King roamed over the north of England. In April, Sir John Hotham refused to admit him into Hull - the city gates remained closed, and in August the King raised his Standard at Nottingham. The Earl of Essex was appointed by Parliament to command their army.

It is not my intention to cover in great detail the British Civil War. I say British because it eventually involved the entire British Isles. It is so often referred to as the *English* Civil War the first fighting was as we have seen between the Scots and their King, it soon engulfed everyone. I shall therefore deal with those events which mattered most to Scotland and where the Scots were considerably involved.

Eighty Peers and 175 members of the English House of Commons had joined Charles and thirty Peers and 300 of the Commons were against him. It must be remembered that the Commons represented, at this time, only about 4% of the population. Sir Edmund Verney echoed the thoughts of the Royalists everywhere when he pronounced "I beseech you .... consider that Majesty is sacred". Also, Charles seemed to the landowners to be the defender of their property against unknown dangers. These fears would prove to be well grounded, as we shall see.

In September 1643, the English Parliamentarians in rebellion against their King signed the Scots' *Solemn League and Covenant.* The war was to be directed by a Committee of both Kingdoms, the Scots being promised £30,000 a month in cash - Cromwell and Pym's Commissioners having raised large loans from Jewish bankers in Amsterdam (the end result of which would be the lifting of the banishment order made when Edward I expelled all Jews from England in 1290). This Committee was the first executive body to be responsible to Parliament, and an assembly of divines was to draw up a plan for the Presbyterian organisations to which a largely Puritan Parliament had now committed the country.

In January 1644 Leslie, now 1st Earl of Leven, led an army of 21,000 Covenanters across the Border, during a heavy snowstorm. Sir Patrick Hepburn of Waughton commanded the East Lothian Regiment. (His sister Isabella had married Sir George Lauder of The Bass who had died in June 1611). The Earl of Balcarre's Regiment had Lieutenants Daniel and Samuel Lauder from the Gunsgreen, Eyemouth, family, cadets of the House of Bass, and one of the two Quartermasters in the Tweeddale Regiment was a Robert Lauder, although it is not clear exactly who he was, but possibly from Lauder.

These regiments were all present at the Battle of Marston Moor, the biggest battle of the war. What appeared at first to be a Royalist success was turned into a route as the combined armies of Scotland (13,000 foot and 2,000 horse), Yorkshire (Sir Thomas Fairfax) and the Eastern Association (the Earl of Manchester and Oliver Cromwell) swept Prince Rupert's Army from the field. Some 6000[79] men were killed or mortally wounded during the battle and pursuit.

150

Whether or not Colonel George Lauder, son of the laird of Haltoun, was in this dreadful battle is not clear. We do know that he was a devout Royalist and intimate friend and companion of William Drummond of Hawthornden who was said to have died of a broken heart at the beheading of his beloved sovereign, Charles I. After the Civil War, George resided at Breda in the Dutch Brabant, and served in the Prince of Orange's army (as did his seven sons). He died in 1670, and his epitaph was written by Sir Alexander Wedderburn.

The Scots, who now announced they wanted peace talks with the King, now quarrelled with Cromwell and his gang, who didn't. and the Scots decided they would return north to storm Newcastle-upon-Tyne, in a particularly bloody encounter. The Earl of Callender had already appeared before Newcastle with a fresh Scots army to reinforce those who had remained behind when the bulk of the army had marched South. Callender steadily bombarded the city and the Earl of Leven arrived back from Marston and eventually completely encircled the city. The garrison inside the walls of Newcastle consisted of only 1,700 men. William Lithgow, a Scottish soldier, left us this account:

> "Now as for the manner of the common souldlers, lying
> here in their severall leagures, and in all parts about the
> towne, their manalons or domiciles, I mean their houts
> are composed, of turff, clay, straw, and watles. Where
> their halls, chambers, kitchines and cellars are all one;
> and yet the better sort (I mean their officers) are
> overshadowed with circulating pavillions, more ready to
> receive the blustring winde then the stinking rain. Then
> at last, all things being orderly done, and their batteries at
> sundrie advantages erected; then (I say) begun they to
> play with cannon and musket at other facers, and often
> also tempering their naked swords in other bloudy bodies:
> where courage cassiering despair, and velour desirous of

---

[79] Gardiner, Samuel, *Hstory of the Great Civil War 1642-49* vol.1, 1987 reprint, , p.382, says 4000 were Royalists.

honour, the exposed themselves unto all hazards and dangerous attempts: neither did they feare death (I meane our owne) more than an auspicious fortune, for being clad with consorts, each provoked another to the uttermost of extremities; and some of them esteeming of the good cause, more than of thewir owne lives, reserved the one and lost the other. So also the oinveterate enemie, making now and the diverse sallies from towne (Issuing at posterne gates) upon our flanking trenches, enhadged themselves into great jeopardies, and our souldlers to as desperat a defence. Where indeed they both often tasted of mutuall fetalitie; till in the end, the Lord Sinclairs Regiment desygned these debording hyrelings a narrower precinct; which was, to keepe their falling bodies more safely within the sheltring walls, which indeed they constrainedly observed. For the enemy within, were more affrayed of the Lord Sinclairs souldlers without, then any one regiment of the army lying about, and they had just reason, recogitating seriously their sanguine blowes and fatall rancounters which they disdainfully felt."

Lithgow had a wholesome respect for the defences of Newcastle which he described as like those of Avignon or Jerusalem. Hunger soon reared its head and divisions began to develop among the townsmen; while outside the Scots, assisted by colliers from Benwell and Elswick, began to mine the town walls and batteries of guns continued to bombard the town preparatory to a final assault. Repeated attempts by the Scots to negotiate a surrender were dismissed by Sir John Marley, the strongly Royalist Mayor. On the 20th October a general attack commenced after a heavy bombardment. The mines were sprung and several breaches made. For two hours scenes of desperate fighting were witnessed but eventually the defenders were overpowered.

King Charles I

Sir John Marley and his officers retreated to the castle itself, but after four days, the situation being so hopeless for them, they surrendered unconditionally.   Marley was then placed in the dungeons but somehow managed to escape, probably with help, to London.   After the final Royalist defeat he went into exile.

In the *Papers Relating to the Scots Army* it is stated that the Reverend John Lauder of Tyninghame[80], a cousin of the new laird, George

---

[80] Where the Lord of the Bass held 1,176 acres. The Lairds of Bass, Waughton, and Scougall, were all present in Tyninghame church on 19th October 1617; and again on 3rd September 1620. Refer: Ritchie, A.E., *The*

Lauder of The Bass (b.1597), had been drafted as one of the Chaplains in the East Lothian Regiment and was present at the battles of Newcastle and Marston Moor. His account[1] of the religious life of the Covenanting Armies gives us a valuable supplement to our knowledge of that period.

The Reverend John Lauder, a graduate of Edinburgh University, was admitted to the charge of Tyninghame – his birthplace – about 1613. The only deviations from his routine as a parish minister that we know of were his stints of duty as an army chaplain – one of the older and most experienced ministers to do so. In November 1638 he attended the Glasgow General Assembly, presumably representing the Presbytery of Haddington who subsequently ordered him to serve in the Second Bishop's War, 1640-41.

He has left us an account of this unhappy time, and mentions the mutiny at Durham on the 19th August 1641, the march to Newcastle the following day, and the subsequent execution by firing squad of the mutineers' leaders on the 25th. He was the last person to address Waughton's Regiment, in the Kirkyard of Dunbar, before it disbanded on Friday 27th. It is clear that no time was lost on the march back to Scotland. Ordered again to serve, he left to join the East Lothian regiment on the 10th November 1645. He returned, from Newcastle via Norham, to Tynninghame on Tuesday 10th March 1646 "in the evening, saiflie, praised be God"[2].

In 1642, James Graham, Marquess of Montrose, who had originally subscribed to the Covenant (in 1638) changed allegiances to King Charles 1st. On the 28th August 1644, Montrose raised the Royal Standard at Blair Athol and with an army of MacDonalds and men of Athol scarcely 3000 strong, took the offensive against the Covenanters and routed them at Tippermuir (lst September 1644), Aberdeen (13th

Churches of Saint Baldred, Edinburgh, 1880, p.166-8, 188.
[1] "The Scottish Historical Review" Ed. Ian B Cowan. Vol. 64, 1985
[2] "Kirk Session Records, Tynninghame", vol. 1, National Records of Scotland.

September), and Inverlochy (2nd February 1645). Now with less than 2000 men, Montrose outmanoeuvred and destroyed an army of 4000 under Sir John Hurry on lst May at Auldearn, two miles east of Nairn.

On the 2nd July the Royal Army defeated the Covenanters again in a fiercely contested battle at Alford, and at Kilsyth on the 15th August Montrose destroyed a Covenanter force of 7000 which had rashly attempted to manoeuvre across the front of the Royalist Army, and little more than 100 of the 6000 of the Covenanters' foot escaped.

Decisive measures were obviously needed by the Parliaments to deal with Montrose, and David Leslie was sent with the Scottish Covenanter Army campaigning in England to track him down. On the 13th September 1645, Leslie surprised and bloodily defeated Montrose's force of 1500 men while they were encamped at Philiphaugh in Selkirkshire.

Leven's regiments had a success the previous year in the action at Corbridge on 19th February 1644, which is worth noting. The Royalists Sir Marmaduke Langdale and Colonel John Fenwick, with 25 troops of horse and three or four hundred musketeers, attacked the regiments of Lord Leven commanded by Lord Balgonie and Lord Kirkudbright, of 15 troops. Both parties drew up between Corbridge and Hexham, and Lieutenant-Colonel James Ballantyne (Leven's Regiment) charged and made the Cavaliers give way with loss. He made a second charge and had taken more than 100 prisoners. Not satisfied, he gave a third charge and drove the Royalists back to their musketeers who were placed behind them, and 'being thus engaged with horse and foote' the Scots 'were disordered and had a very strait retreat through a gap, where some men were lost...'

The Cavaliers did not pursue far, perhaps because they were 'loath to engage beyond their foot notwithstanding their advantage.' The Scots wheeling in disorder were met by Colonel Robert Brandling, who with 10 more troops had crossed the the river Tyne below Corbridge, in order to fall on the rear of the Scots and in fact ran into their front as they fell back. 'Brandling forwardly rode out before his Troupes to exchange a Pistoll, and only lieutenant Elliot (Leven's Regiment) rode up to him, and when they had discharged each at other, and were wheeling about to draw their swords, Brandling's horse stumbled, and the Lieutenant was so neere him as to pull him off his horse,…..' Seeing this Brandling's men retreated, which gave the Scots courage to fall on and drive them back over the river where they killed some and 'forced others through the water so hastily, that there were even some of them drowned…'

The Scots claimed that honours were even, and that in all about 60 men were killed. The Duke of Newcastle in a dispatch to the King (9th March) asserted that Langdale had won the day, putting the Scots losses at 200 killed and 150 wounded or taken. However, it is not very likely that the Scots lost the equivalent of five full troops in an affair of this sort. The claim that Langdale's men took two cornets and a guidon may, however, be accepted. The prisoners included Major Agnew, Captain Arthur Forbes and QM Archibald Mackay from Lord Kirkudbright's regiment, a Captain Haddon and his Cornet, Ker, (grandson of Lord Roxburgh) while Lord Balgonie was shot through the shoulder. The Royalists lost Colonel Brandling and a lieutenant, 'none else of note.' While Langdale was attacking Corbridge Colonel Sir Gamaliel Dudley from his quarters at Prudhoe crossed the Tyne and with some horse and dragoons and attacked a Scots quarter with such success that they abandoned four others in the neighbourhood.

Following the fall of Oxford in June 1646, King Charles had given himself up to the Scots. Some said at the time that "to their everlasting shame", they handed him over to the English Parliament on the 30th January, 1647. However, as with all revolts, the victors had now begun arguing amongst themselves on a whole range of policies. The King was in the Parliamentary Army's custody at Hampton Court from where, on the 11th November, 1647, he escaped and fled to the Isle of Wight. There, on the 26th December, Charles signed an *Agreement* with the Scottish Commissioners from London in which he agreed to accept Presbyterianism for at least three years in England.

It is recorded that Richard Lauder Lord of Haltoun, (father-in-law of Charles Maitland, 3rd Earl of Lauderdale and therefore progenitor of today's Earl) was a Member of Parliament for Edinburghshire, a Commissioner for Excise, and sat on the Committees of War in Edinburgh in both 1647 and 1648, the deliberations of which led to a new Royal Scottish Army entering England in July 1648. But it was an army led by James, Duke of Hamilton and the nobility, not the disciplined army of the Covenant.

The Journals of Sir John Lauder, Lord Fountainhall 1665-1676 mention that one of the sons of Sir Lewis Lauder of Adinstoun ("a son of the old Laird of Haltoun and Bellenden of Broughton", who had married a daughter of Sir Archibald Acheson, Secretary of Scotland), had joined "the Kings Troop". Sir John Foulis of Ravelston records him living in February 1698 when they were hunting together at Ratho.

Cromwell met Hamilton in August and in a long, straggling battle between Preston and Warrington won the greatest of his victories.
He was outnumbered by three to one, but he attacked the Scots in detail and completely routed them, killing and capturing some 5000. The Scottish horse had managed to escape but were hunted down by John Lambert, and Hamilton was captured at Uttoxeter.

King Charles I was executed, aged 48, in Whitehall, London, on the 30th January,1649.

Chapter 11

DUNBAR

An Act of Settlement of Ireland (12th August 1652) provided for the expropriation of the owners of some two thirds of the land. This was never fully carried out, but a great deal of Irish land passed to traitorous London merchants who had lent money to the Parliamentary cause. This pattern would be, albeit to a lesser extent, repeated in Scotland, where clear lines were being drawn between devout Royalists and those prepared to betray the legitimate cause for retention of their lands, their titles, or simply for profit.

In the early months of 1649 the Rump of the Long Parliament at Westminster passed laws to make England a republic. The Scottish Parliament did not agree to this and it is noted that the Member for Lauder in 1649 was William Lauder in Park [Winepark] whose estate was outside Lauder in Berwickshire, a cadet of the House of Bass.

Cromwell returned to England in May 1650, following a vicious and bloodthirsty pacification of Ireland. Intelligence relayed to him showed that the Royalist cause was gathering strength again in Scotland. Montrose tried to raise the Highlands for the young Charles II, who landed in Scotland in June and he was proclaimed King in July. Montrose, however, was betrayed by Macleod of Assynt and was defeated at Carbisdale.

Cromwell marched north with 5,000 horse and 10,000 foot, the vast majority of them veterans. After reprovisioning at Dunbar, Cromwell made contact with a Scottish Army in excess of 20,000 men under David Leslie on the 29th July. The Scots were deployed in an exceptionally strong position between Edinburgh and Leith, and in appalling weather conditions the New Model Army retreated to Musselburgh and then back to Dunbar. It was a fighting withdrawal, for the Scots had attacked the army's quarters at Musselburgh and harried the rearguard.

Already between 4000 and 5000 of Cromwell's troops were sick, and it was imperative that he bring about a battle before his army wasted away. Cromwell again advanced and attempted to turn the right flank of the Scots position but Leslie was equal to this manoeuvre and the New Model Army returned to Dunbar on the lst September.

During this time, according to a manuscript volume in the Advocate's Library, whilst the English foraged for food in the district, the following incident occurred: "when Oliver Cromwell, that grand usurper hypocrite and great wicked man, lay with his army encamped about Dunbar, before the battle of Doon-hill, he sent a party to North Berwick, where the Laird of Bass had a house, with barnyard and other offices. The party entered the barn, where the corn was sacked up ready to be carried out to be sown, the party having offered to carry off the corn for use by their master, the Lord Protector (as they called him) and his army, the Laird's servant went into the house and acquainted Mistress Margaret, the old Laird's sister, who had the management of his family affairs. She immediately ordered the sharpest knife and a flail to be brought to her, and went into the barn, where, after upbraiding the men, she ripped up the sacks, and managed the flail with such dexterity that she beat off the party; for which she most deservedly may be accounted amongst the greatest and most glorious heroines of that Age. George Lauder of The Bass was obliged to abscond *"because he was a Royalist, as all of that and other families of that name have almost always been, and still continue"*.

The Scottish Army now advanced and deployed on a strong position on Doon Hill, effectively cutting the land route to England. Cromwell would have to evacuate his army by the sea or fight his way out of encirclement. Equally, Leslie would have to attack if he was not to see his prey slip away on board the English fleet. The Scots' deployment extended inland from the coast for over 3000 yards with the majority of their troops positioned on the forward slope of Doon Hill, between the summit and the Brox burn After reconnoitring the Scots position, Cromwell and Lambert judged it to be vulnerable, and between 5am and 6 am the next morning Lambert, with six regiments of horse and Monck, with just over three regiments of foot, charged and surprised the Scottish right. The Scots nevertheless defended fiercely until the arrival of Cromwell with with a reserve of horse and foot, which cut through the Scots right and began to roll up their line. The centre and left of Leslie's army disintegrated in surrender or flight and the Horse of the New Model set off in pursuit. With 3000 Scots killed and over 10,000 captured Leslie's army had been almost wiped out.

Layout for the Battle of Dunbar in 1650

Cromwell pursued Leslie and the remains of his army to Stirling, but the Parliamentarian forces were not strong enough to risk an assault on the town's fortifications. Cromwell withdrew to Edinburgh and for the next eight months the Scots and the English, both too weak to risk a decisive battle, skirmished with each other, and the weather.

George Lauder had transferred his fortress of The Bass to his uncle, Sir Patrick Hepburn of Waughton. The Lauders being renowned monarchists, and Sir Patrick having commanded the East Lothian Regiment in England in the Covenanters army, it was felt by George that by this move Cromwell would not confiscate the Lauders ancient seat. However, Sir Patrick subsequently unexpectedly died, and on 9th November 1649 his son John was served heir to the feudal Barony of The Bass. He was a former Episcopalian minister - and a Royalist.

While Cromwell established his headquarters in Edinburgh several supply ships left Dunbar en-route for Leith. One of these ships, the "John 'o London", contained all of Cromwell's personal luggage. In the early hours, as they attempted to sail quietly past the Castle of the Bass, which guarded the approaches to the Forth from the South, all hell suddenly broke loose as a full artillery barrage let loose at almost point blank range. The garrison, forewarned, had been waiting. Two ships were sunk, including Cromwell's baggage ship. Furious, Cromwell caused large notices to appear in all towns and villages along the East Lothian coast threatening death by hanging to anyone found to be taking supplies of any kind to the Bass:

Proclamation against Intercourse with the Garrison of the Bass
By the Governour of Edinburgh, Leith, and Berwick

Whereas I am informed that divers persons, both on the South and North

162

*side of the Firth, do aswel receive the
Boats of the Bass coming from thence,
and supply them with necessaries, and
also send in Boats with Provisions to the
same: These are therefore to give notice
to all persons whatsoever, That whoever
from henceforth shall hold any
corresponcie with any in the Bass, or
entertain any company from thence, or
afford them any provision, or hold any
other correspondencie, with them
whatsoever, shall forfeit all their goods,
and be tryed at a Court Martiall for their
lives, as Correspondents with the Enemy.*

*Given under my hand and seal at Leith,
Sept. 6, 1651*

G. Fenwick.

*This to be proclaimed in the severall Towns
on both sides of the Firth, by beat of Drum.*

Extracts from 'Mercurius Scoticus'
Thursday (Oct. 16).

*This day at a Court Martiall at Leith it was
Ordered that Andrew Bennett, Master of a
Boat belonging to the Ferry neer Ely (for that
it appeared he was commanded in, and
forced to submit to some of the Enemy in the
Boat belonging to Bass Island), shall have his
Boat and Goods restored but for his carrying
of Souldiers without a Pass, shall forfeit
twenty shillings sterling, to be paid to*

Captain Roleston, to be by him distributed
amongst his Souldiers that took them.

(Wednesday, Oct. 22.)
This day also a Summons issued from the
Honourable the Deputy-Governor of Leith,
for surrender of Bass Island, thus:-

Sir, - I desire you upon sight hereof, to
deliver into the possession of Captain
Roleston, The Bass Island, with all the Forts,
Fortifications, Ordnance, Arms, Ammunition,
Provisions, Magazens, and Stores therein, for
the use of the Parliament of England, to
avoid the effusion of bloud, or destruction,
which may otherwise happen.   This if you
shall think fit to embrace, you will render
yourself sensible of your own good, and you
(with the Forces with you) shall receive such
Conditions as shall be fit for you to accept,
and me to grant: I am, Your servant,
Timo. Wilks.
Leith, Octob. 22, 1651.

To the Chief Commander of Bass Island,
these.

Thursday (Oct. 23)
A Party of Horse that were Ordered forth
with   Commissioner   Desbrough   for
apprehending the Wife and Brothers of the
Governour of the Bass Island (for relieving
him with all Necessaries),
brough[t] the said Parties prisoners to Leith
Garrison, whence they are to be shipt away
by the first conveniencie, except the

Governour of the Island shall upon notice thereof seek reasonable terms, and apply himself timely for their remedy.

Saturday (Oct. 25).
This day also, the Lady, [Hepburn of Waughton and Redbraes] *and two Brothers of the Governour of the Bass Island, were by Order of the Deputy Governour sent aboard the* Admirall, *to be disposed of there till further Order. Likewise their Father and they are to be sent to London, and their Estates sequestered, unless the Bass shall be suddenly rendred. In order to which the Lady hath wrote a Letter to her Husband, with pregnant Arguments (as all Places in these parts have found favour by rendition, and shee being great with Childe, together with other miseries which else may befall him and them) importuning him to yeeld it; the return is not yet come; but without doubt he (if considerate and ingenious) will not stand out.*

Eventually, in April 1652, the garrison of 112 men were starved, and frozen out. An interesting note from the *Expenses of the English Army*, in April 1653, published in *Scotland and the Commonwealth*, shows that £6-0-0 was allotted to the Bass for "Fire and Candle".

By June 1651 both sides had been reinforced, and Charles II's army was now an irascible blend of his Scots and English supporters numbering some 20,000. In August 1651 the Royalist Army crossed the Border, the ultimate aim being London. Cromwell, who had been busy capturing Perth, now set off in pursuit. Charles, harried all the way south by Lambert & Major-General Harrison with half a dozen regiments of Parliamentary horse, finally reached Worcester on the 22nd August, his army now exhausted and down to 16,000.

The King himself fought bravely in the ensuing battle, leading an attack on the 3rd September on the Parliamentarians on the River Teme. However, the battle was lost and Charles was forced to flee to France. Stuart military power in Britain had been unequivocally crushed.

In July 1653 Cromwell, having abolished the Long Parliament (which had sold Crown, Dean and Chapter lands, and the lands of some 700 Royalists for a song) established a new, appointed body, sometimes known as the 'Barebones Parliament'. Reforms spewed out of this gathering. However, from the point of view of the great feudal landowners of Scotland the most serious reform was the abolition of tithes.

The compromised Rev. John Hepburn of Waughton had hurriedly re-transferred The Bass to his only daughter and heiress Margaret, but alas Cromwell's Commissioners were not to be fooled by these manoeuvres and on the 2nd July 1655 the *Barony of Bass* was confiscated by State Commissioners William Hog and George Norvell. After 600 years, the Lauders had lost their island fortress.

It later became, in turn, a prison for Covenanters and a fortress under James II. It was the last castle in Scotland to fall to the Glorious Revolution, and was disarmed and abandoned thereafter. It was sold by the Crown for one penny in 1706 to Sir Hew Dalrymple Bt., (cr.1664) whose merchant family had done well during the Civil War. They had previously purchased, in 1700, the Barony of North Berwick.

EPILOGUE

During the century leading up to the Civil War the Lauders became increasingly impoverished supporting the monarchist cause with loans, paying growing taxes, and supporting the now oppressive Kirk, not to mention supplying men for the never-ending wars and therefore neglecting their estates.

There is a *Deed of Obligation*[81] by Mary Queen of Scots and Darnley whereby they promise to repay Robert Lauder of The Bass the £2000 (a huge sum at that time) that he had loaned then in 1566. This did not happen and one of those who went surety for the debt, Sir John Stewart, the Laird of Traquhair, was summoned by Lady Bass, whereby a decision was given against him at Stirling Castle on the 21st March 1579 by the Lords of Council and Session. There is no record, however, that he ever paid up. Probably he would not have been able to. The other three sureties were already dead.

In 1593 the Barony and town of Tyninghame, the lordship bailiery and manor thereof, and the office of heritable justiciar, were re-ratified to Sir George Lauder of Bass and his heirs in a very splendid Charter to be found in *Acta Parliamentorum, Jacobi VI* , and gives full details of the very extensive family possessions as at that date. Thomas Hannan[82], says of Tyninghame: "exactly how old was the house it is difficult to say, but there was a house on the lands in 1094, in the days of King Duncan (II), when it was owned by the lairds of Bass". The Bishops of St Andrews, who, at the invitation of the Laird, used it as a country residence as early as the 13th Century made additions to it, and, Hannan says, "in 1617 Isabella Hepburn (mother of the then Laird, George Lauder of Bass), the Lady of the Bass, made further additions". However, it would appear that as the new century progressed that financial difficulties forced the Lauders to mortgage Tyninghame and a sale was forced in 1628 to John, Lord Murray of

---

[81] *Register of Deeds*, vol. viii No. 279.
[82] *Famous Scottish Houses*, 1928.

Lochmaben (afterwards the new Earl of Annandale, [cr.1662]) 'for 200,000 merkes'. Lady Bass was evicted from her lovely home, the ancient Manor. A mystery surrounds this state of affairs as when Sir George Lauder of Bass died on 27th June 1611, he left the then huge sum of £29,175 including 'moveables' and exclusive of landed estates.

Seven years later, in 1635, Lord Murray resold Tyninghame to the first Earl of Haddington (cr.1619) for the same sum. Several years ago, Alexander Hay, the laird of Duns in Berwickshire, told me that he recalled seeing, in his youth, books that were inscribed *Lauder of Bass* at his home in Duns Castle. These books almost certainly originated from the library at Tyninghame. The Haddingtons eventually sold Tyninghame in 1987.[1]

In 1652 Richard Lauder of Haltoun's daughter, Elizabeth, married the Hon. Charles Maitland, later the 3rd Earl of Lauderdale (cr.1624). His brother was the notorious Duke, and it was through this marriage that the Barony and large estates of Haltoun became one of the chief possessions of the Maitlands. AG Bradley states, in *Gateway to Scotland,* that the Lauders were driven out of Lauder by the Maitlands but there is no evidence to support this.

On the 2nd April 1550, an Order in Council had decreed that the forts at Lauder, Dunglas, Roxburgh & Eyemouth be demolished, several of them being, at that time, invested by the English. However, following the expulsion (with French assistance) of the English from Lauder fort on the 20th April nothing appears to have been done and the property was returned to George Wedderat and his wife Alison Lauder, to whom it had been conveyed in 1532 probably as dowry.

---

[1] The contents were auctioned on the 28th and 29th September 1987, and it was disappointing to note that Sotheby's, in their sumptuous hard-cover book-catalogue, failed to mention the Lauders in their summary of the history of the house.

168

Bitter family feuds being the norm rather than the exception at that time, George Wedderat was "slaughtered" by Gilbert Lauder of Balbardie & Whitslaid, with other relatives, in September 1565, at Wedderat's residence near Lauder Burn. In 1583 the dead man's son sold the fort to Thomas Cranstoun and, in 1586, he sold it to Sir John Maitland of Thirlestane. The Lauders and the Maitlands were both intermarried with the Cranstouns.

Haltoun, at Ratho, a seat of the Lauder family

The Maitlands of Thirlestane were another great feudal family, their Pele Tower of that designation being 2 miles east of Lauder,[2] but their

---

[2] Prior to the de Morville properties passing to the Douglases, the lands of Thirlestane were granted to Alan, a vassal. His granddaughter, Alicia, carried

main residence becameLethington (now Lennoxlove) near Haddington, which they acquired by marriage with a Giffard heiress. Sir John was now Chancellor and had control of the nation's purse strings. He curried favour with James VI who made him Lord Thirlestane in 1590. His immediate successors were Viscount Lauderdale in 1616 and 1st Earl of Lauderdale in 1624.

Upon the old fort at Lauder Lord Thirlestane commenced building the great edifice that we see today - Thirlestane Castle. The original Tower at Thirlestane was abandoned. Its partial ruins may still be seen today below the tiny hamlet bearing that name. The Maitlands supported the Union of Crowns and Parliaments were no strangers to intrigue throughout the 17th century. With the accumulation of wealth and favour that century the Maitlands would go on to buy up what they had not acquired by the traditional border method - feuding.

It seems that the almost constant feuding wore the Lauders of Lauder down, and their prestige itself would have been damaged by the erection at the very edge of their lands and burgh of a magnificent palace. Others coveted their ancient hegemony and hereditary rights.

In October 1594, Gilbert Lauder, a supporter of Bothwell and brother of the laird of Whitslaid, was murdered by John Cranstoun of Corsbie, at Linlithgow. And on the day before Christmas 1595, William Cranstoun of that Ilk murdered Andrew Lauder of Wyndpark, a Pele Tower above Earnscleugh Water, slightly north east of the town.

---

by marriage Thirlestane to Richard de Mautelant (Maitland), founder of the present house. It is thought that the Maitlands came to Britain with William the Conqueror - 10 years after the Lauders came to Scotland. In *The Story of the Tweed* Sir Herbert Maxwell states: "Previous to the Maitlands obtaining ascendancy in Lauderdale, there was another family of landowners there named Lauder of that Ilk. They had several towers in the district: the ruins of one may be seen on the left bank of the Leader Water at Whitslaid, a couple of miles below Lauder."

Late in February 1598 the Lady Marischal, Lord Home's sister, gave a reception and the Lauders were amongst those on the invitation list. Unfortunately so were the Cranstouns. A dreadful vitriolic row broke out with terrible abuse being used angrily in front of the hostess by the Lauders. Lord Home, seeking redress for the insult to his sister, sought revenge and agreed to assist the Cranstouns in their feud. The affair came to a head on the 10th May 1598.

Robert Lauder of that Ilk and his two kinsmen, William "of the West Port" (the western gatehouse to the town, near where Middle Row is today) and James Lauder, were dispensing justice, in their roles as hereditary bailies, in the still extant Tolbooth in Lauder. Suddenly a party of Cranstouns and Humes, led by Lord Home, descended on the burgh courthouse seeking William Lauder. During their attempt to break down the door William managed to fire a pistol from a small window, killing John Cranstoun. He then tried to escape through a side door but was caught by his pursuers and hacked to pieces. James and Robert Lauder of that Ilk were "dirked while on the bench".

The West Port of the Royal Burgh of Lauder, through which passed many armies of all sides

The Presbytery at Haddington subsequently excommunicated Lord Home "for the slaughter of William Lauder" and the matter was referred to James VI who was inclined to shudder before the powerful

Home clan. He therefore placed the matter in the hands of Sir Thomas Erskine, Sir George Home and Nicholas Cairncross. In the meantime Home's sister, the Lady Marischal, had died. [83]

Sir John Lauder, Lord Fountainhall, says in his *MS Excerpts from the Criminal Registers* that "the King pardoned the said Earl [in the meantime, in 1605, Home had been made an Earl!] as he had satisfied the said burgh (by financial reparations) for the said slaughter and burning".

Robert Lauder of that Ilk had been married to Margaret, daughter of William II Borthwick of Soutra & Johnstonburn (d.1563) by his spouse Katherine Crichton. Robert never recovered from his wounds and was buried in the 'auld kirk' near the Fort at Lauder (now Thirlestane Castle) leaving Margaret with seven young children. The Lauders and Borthwicks had been allies for centuries. Sir Alexander Lauder of Haltoun, who was killed at the Battle of Pinkie, had been married to Janet, daughter of William, 5th Lord Borthwick. Borthwick Castle remains one of the best preserved castles in the Borders and Nisbet says that it is "after the Hungarian form" and that the first of this ancient and noble family came from Hungary to Scotland, in the retinue of Queen Margaret, in the reign of Malcolm Canmore. However, Hannan (1928) asserts that "the origin of the family of Borthwick is attributed to a Lord of Burtick in Livonia." If this latter statement is correct, that barony was on the eastern shores of lake Burtneiku ezers (modern spelling) west of the town of Walk (Valka) in Estonia.

Robert's immediate heir, another Robert and Justice of the Peace for Berwickshire, continued the Lauder feuds with the Homes, but is noted about 1627: "Robert Lauder of that Ilk is cautioned that he should attend the Goodman [William Borthwick] of Johnstonburn till they were all in readiness to goe off the country to serve in the wars."[84]

---

[83] Mackie, J.D., LL.D., etc., editor, *Calendar of the State Papers relating to Scotland 1547-1603,* Edinburgh, 1969, vol. xiii, Part 1, number 156, pps: 205-208 and 214.

Which wars these are is unclear but possibly for Sweden. This Colonel William Borthwick had been in the service of King Gustavus Adolphus, and served at the battle of Lutzen in 1632.

In *The Register of the Privy Council of Scotland*[85] there is an entry dated 2nd October 1627, in which certain fugitives are mentioned escaping the baillies at Lauder, one of whom went *towardis the Laird of Lauderis tour [tower] and place*. In 1629 Messrs C Lowther, R Fallon and Peter Manson thus wrote in their *Journal of their Tour in Scotland*: "In Lauder dwell many of the Lauders, one of whose houses is a very fine one". This is certainly a reference to Lauder Tower.

Robert's son and heir, dying in his lifetime, meant that he later left his lands and forest of Lauder to his daughter, Isobel, who had married Alexander Home of St Leonards, south of Lauder. Alexander and his brother Harry were both burgesses of Lauder. She is recorded as having sold or feued them on to the Earl of Lauderdale. It is difficult to understand how this arrangement could have come about as Isobel's father had three brothers. William, living in 1643 and recorded in many documents with his elder brother Robert, John (living 1620), and Richard Lauder in Allanshaws, nr.Lauder (living 1657).

However by the end of the century the great buttressed Tower lay deserted and we note from the *Lauderdale Accounts* that the foundations of the tower were dug up between December 1699 and February 1701, the mason employed in the demolition being Mr James Bennett. Robert Romanes, writing in his *Papers on Lauder* in 1903, said that Tower Yard was then still in existence next to the Free Kirk Manse and county police station. The Lauder Tower at Whitslaid fared better, it being out of town, and apart from the roof was intact in the 19th century. It has partially collapsed topday although remains of it are still visible. On The Bass the residential quarters of the castle were taken down in 1902 so that the stone could be used to build the lighthouse. The castle walls are still there as are the ruins of the chapel and, amazingly, the landing place.

---

[84] Stewart-Smith, 1898, p.279-280.
[85] Vol.viii, 1644-1660, Edinburgh,1908, p. 420.

The Lauders were a great feudal entity. Their wealth depended upon their baronies and estates like all great landed families. They fought long and hard over 600 years for their monarchs with a dedication that would be hard to equal. Because their loyalty was so reliable, Kings felt no need to bribe them with titles. Any student of Scottish creations will be surprised at the number of titles so granted by a monarch, afraid of a particular magnate's power being used against him. The ironical thing is that very often, even after the new ennoblements, that is exactly what happened.

The other interesting study to be made is that of titles awarded in the century after the Union of Crowns in 1603. James VI was weak and easily manipulated by courtiers. Political corruption and bribes were the norm in that century. Many of the recipients of new titles would betray their monarchs, and Scottish independence, fought for so many centuries at such vast cost. I recommend a glance at *1707 - The Union of Scotland and England*. This compact study outlines the corruption and bribery in this vital last century of Scottish sovereignty.

The most profound comment on this sorry period (17th century) of Scottish history comes, ironically, from Sir John Lauder, 2nd Bt., Lord Fountainhall, writing in 1672:

"The old nobility cannot but repute them selfes slighted when they sie thesse great offices of State conferred upon upstarts. But this is a part of the absolute power of Kings, to raise men from the dunghill and make them their oune companions."

Scottish history did not commence in 1603. There are other families like the Lauders, who are all but forgotten today. Sir Herbert Maxwell, in *The Story of the Tweed*, laments the fate of the ancient aristocracy when he wrote of "the great feudal families, how many have disappeared".

174

Even in 19th century histories there is often scant mention, such books often glorifying the roles of the newer aristocracy in order to bolster their position in society, particularly prevalent in that century, many of the 19th century histories being sponsored by patrons, whose ancestors hardly appear in pre-Union Scottish history. Clearly this period history needs re-researching and rewriting, so that the credit due is given to those who provided invaluable services to the Scottish nation.

The chief Lauder family representative today is Sir Piers Dick Lauder whose ancestor became a Baronet of Nova Scotia in 1688. He is a descendant of Sir Robert de Lawedre who entered Scotland with Siward in the service of Malcolm Canmore in 1054.

THE OATH OF A KNIGHT

I shall fortify and defend the true, Holy
Catholick and Christian Religion
presently professed, at all my Power.

I shall be loyal and true to my Sovereign
Lord the King His Majesty, and do Honour
and Reverence to all Orders of Chivalry, and
to the noble Office of Arms.

I shall fortify and defend Justice to the
uttermost of my Power, without Feud or
Favour.

I shall never fly from the King's Majesty my
Lord and Master, or his Lieutenant In Time
of Battel, or Medly with Dishonour.

I shall defend my native Country from all
Aliens and Strangers at all my Power.

I shall maintain and defend the honest Adoes
and Quarrels of all Ladies of Honour,
Widows, Orphans, and Maids of good Fame.

I shall do Diligence wherever I hear tell
there are any Traitors, Murderers, Rovers,
and Masterful Thieves and Outlaws,
that suppress the Poor, to bring them to the
Law at all my power.

I shall maintain and defend the Noble and
gallant State of Chivalry with Horses,
Harnesses, and other Knightly apparel to my
Power.

I shall be diligent to enquire and seek to have
the knowledge of all Articles and Points
touching or concerning my Duty, in the
Book of Chivalry.

All and sundry the Premisses I oblige me to
keep and fulfil. So help me God; by my own
hand, and by God himself.

From: *The Works of William Drummond of Hawthornden.*

*There lay he, mighty and mightily fallen,
done with his gallantry.*

Homer

Whence hath fled thine ancient glory?

J.Stewart Smith, in
The Grange of St.Giles.

APPENDIX I - BIBLIOGRAPHY

The History of Dunbar by James Miller (Haddington 1830)

The Spottiswoode Miscellany 2 vols. (Edinburgh 1844)

The Bass Rock by Messrs. McCrie, Miller, Anderson, Fleming and Balfour (Edinburgh, 1847)

The History of Scotland by PF Tytler. 10 vols. (Edinburgh,1866)

The Swintons of that Ilk & their Cadets (Edinburgh 1883)

Notes on Historical References to the Scottish Family of Lauder. Edited by James Young (Glasgow 1884)

The House of Cockburn of that Ilk, & The Cadets Thereof by Thomas H Cockburn-Hood (Edinburgh 1888)

Memorials of the Earls of Haddington, by Sir William Fraser, 2 vols. (Edinburgh 1889)

A History of the Scottish People by the Rev.Thomas Thomson. 6 vols. (Edinburgh,1893)

The Grange of St Giles by J Stewart Smith (Edinburgh,1898)

Journals of Sir John Lauder, Lord Fountainhall 1665 - 1676 (Edinburgh 1900)

Lauder and Lauderdale, by A Thomson (Galashiels 1902)

The Scots Peerage Edited by Sir James Balfour Paul (1905)

Papers on Lauder by Robert Romanes (1903)

The Story of the Tweed by Sir Herbert Maxwell, Bart. (London 1909)

The Gateway of Scotland by A.G.Bradley (London, 1912)

The Berwick and Lothian Coasts by Ian C Hannan (1913)

Famous Scottish Houses - The Lowlands by Thomas Hannan (London 1928)

Brave Borderland by H Drummond Gould (London 1934)

The Tudors and Stuarts by MM Reese (London, 1940/1971 reprint)

The Bass Rock in History in *Transactions of the East Lothian Antiquarian and Field Naturalists Society,* 5th Vol. 1948

The Century of Revolution 1603-1714 by Christopher Hill (London, 1961/1991 reprint)

Scotland under Mary Stuart by Madeleine Bingham (London 1971)

The Stewart Kingdom of Scotland 1371-1603 by Caroline Bingham (London 1974)

1707 - The Union of Scotland and England by P. H. Scott (Edinburgh 1979)

The Anglo-Norman Era in Scottish History by Professor G.W.S. Barrow, Clarendon Press Oxford, 1980.

The North Berwick Story by Walter M Ferrier (North Berwick 1981)

Periods In Highland History by Messrs. Grant and Cheape (London,1987)

The Protocol Book, Lauder 1543-1553, of Robert Wedderop, Notary, Edited by T Maley & W Elliot (Selkirk, 1993)

Marston Moor 1644 – The Campaign and The Battle, by Peter Young
(Moreton-in-Marsh, Gloucestershire, 1998)

APPENDIX II - EXTRACTS FROM: *Documents Relating to Scotland Preserved in Her Majesty's Public Record Office, London.* Edited by Joseph Bain, FSA (Scot.) Vol. IV, AD 1357 - 1509. Published by HM General Register House, Edinburgh 1888.

October 26th 1398   510. Indenture (in vernacular) at Haudenstank between Sir William of Borthwic, Sir John of Remorgny, knights, and Adam Forstar esquire, commissioners for Scotland, and Sir John Bussey and three others, commissioners for England, agreeing for the return of prisoners and ransoms and the due observance of the truce. The Earl of March Warden of the East March for Scotland, and Sir Henry Percy warden for England, are bound for same by their respective letters. Sir Richard of Rothirfurde, Sir William Stewart, knights, Walter Scot, Thomas Tornebule, and **Robert de Lawedre**[1] are 'borowis' for the Earl of Douglas's bounds on the Middle March. Sir Thomas Gray of Heton, Sir Thomas Grey of Horton,knights, Robert of Umfraville, John of Mydforde, and Thomas of Knayton are 'borowis' for Sir Henry Percy's bounds for the East March. Adam of Gordon, William the Barde, and Adam Franche are excepted from the free delivery of prisoners, and bound under the pledge of the Scottish Commissioners, to appear and render themselves at the next meeting of the Great Commissioners under a penalty of *3000l.* to answer for the *'unmesurit harmes'* done by them as common truce breakers. [*Chapter House (Scots Docts.) Box 95, No. 2*].

Much defaced and blackened with galls. Three seals in red wax, and much damaged and flattened, appended. (1) Couche, 3   cinquefoils, 2 and 1. Crest and legend obliterated. Supporters, 2 lions sejant (Sir William Borthwick). (2) Signet, an otter's (?) head couped. Above, a star of 8 rays between a pair of stag's horns (Sir John Ramorgny). (3) Oval. Beneath a canopy a mitred abbottseated,a crook in his right hand, in pale. *Leg.* (illegible). (The Abbott of Melros, whose seal is said to be appended.)

April 20th 1408 754. The K. grants safe conduct and protection to **Master William of Lawdre** archdeacon of Lothian[2], George of

---

[1] Son of Alan Lauder of that Ilk and Alicia Campbell. Present at the battles of Otterburn and Nesbit Moor. Died 1425.
[2] Bishop of Glasgow and in 1423 Chancellor of Scotland. Died 1425.

Borthwyke clerk, and Master Alexander of Lillescliffe, with twelve horsemen coming from France to Scotland, and returning to France, till Pentecost next. Pontefract Castle.

[*Patent, 1-11 Hen. IV. m. 6.*]

December 1st 1412 833. Warrant to the Chancellor for safe conduct (in the form enclosed) till Pentecost following, for William 'Sire de Graham, 'Mestre Robert de Lany licenciez en decrees prevost de Seint 'Andrew, William de Borthwik esquier, et **George de Lawedre** 'burgeys', [Burgess][3] ambassadors appointed by the Council General of Scotland to treat for the deliverance of James K. of Scotland and for truce, as signified in letters from the high and puissant prince the Duke of Albany the K.'s very dear cousin, with 40 horsemen in their company. Westminster. (Enclosure) [*Privy Seals (Tower), 14 Hen. IV. File 3.*]

May 13th 1423 926. Agreed in Council at Westminster to grant a safe conduct for half a year, for **Master Alexander of Lawedre dean of Dunkeld**[4] in Scotland, and his retinue of eight persons, to come and go between Flanders and England. The lords present, the Dukes of Gloucester and Exeter, the Archbishop of Canterbury, the Bishops of Wynton, Norwich, and Worcester, the Earl of Warwick, Fitz Hugh, Cromewelle, Tiptoft, the Chancellor and Treasurer.

Same day and place, another for same period, for **George Lawedre**[5] **and Robert Lawedre of   Scotland**, for their ship laden with fish and other merchandise between England and their own   country. Present the Lords of Council *ut supra*. [*Tower Miscellaneous Rolls, No. 459.*]

August 19th 1423 932. Commission by Murdac duke of Albany earl of Fife and Menteth and Governor of Scotland, to **William**[6] **bishop of Glasgow chancellor of Scotland**, George earl of March, James of

---

[3] George Lauder of Haltoun, a burgess and Provost of Edinburgh.
[4] Alexander was a brother of William, Bishop of Glasgow. He became Bishop of Dunkeld in May 1440 and died that year.
[5] The same George the 'burgess' mentioned in the safe-conduct of 1st December 1412.
[6] As note 2.

Douglas of Balvani his brother, the Abbots of Cambuskineth and Balmurinach, Sir Patrick of Dunbar of Bele, **Sir Robert de Lawedre of Edringtron, knights**[7] , Master George of Borthwike archdeacon of Glasgow, and Master Patrick of Houston licentiate in laws, canon of Glasgow his secretary, ambassadors to treat for the liberation of James K. of Scotland. Given inder the Great seal of his office at the town of Innerkethyne 19th August 1423, 3rd of his government. [*Chapter House (Scots Docts.), Box 96, No. 17.*]

Fragment of a fine seal, in white wax, appended. Obv. The Governor in a chair of state, a drawn sword in right hand, his left on breast; a lion at each side of chair. Shield at his left with arms of Albany (as in No. 793). *Rev.* Lower half of a mailed figure riding to sinister. Lion and Tressure on surcoat and housings; quatrefoils in field. *Leg.* (broken off).

Sept. 10th 1423 933. Treaty in the Chapter House, York, on 10th September 1423, between the English ambassadors and seven of those of Scotland (excepting the Earl of March and James Douglas of Balvany) for the liberation of James K. of Scots, who will pay 40,000 *l.* English money for his maintenance in England, and contract marriage with some high-born English lady. [*Chapter House (Scots Docts.), Box 93, No. 11.*]

Seven seals, in red wax, appended. (1) Round; half figure of a bishop, mitred and vested, under a canaopy: 's' WIL'MI EP'I GLASGUENSIS.' (2) Oval, broken; the coronation of the B.V.Mary: 's' . . . DE . . . . BUSKIN . . . . (Abbot of Cambuskenneth). (3) Fragment of signet. (4) Signet; a star of 6 rays, wavy. (5) Fragment of signet. (6) Signet; a griffin's head and neck (**Lawder**?). (7) Round; under a canopy a figure standing with raised sword; some indistinct object at his feet (St. Michael?). A small shield below (defaced): 's' PATRICH DE HOUSTON.'

December 4th 1423 940. Warrant for safe conduct till 1st March next to John of Touris, **George de Lawedre, Robert de Lawedre**[1],

---

[7] This Sir Robert was the grandson of Alan Lauder of that Ilk. Edrington Castle was above the Whiteadder river near Berwick.

[1] Probably Sir Robert Lauder of Edrington (d.1451) or his father, George's brother.

184

and James Rede, at present in England, and two servants each, to go to Scotland and return at pleasure. Westminster.
Similar for **Gilbert de Lawedre** and four servants. [*Privy Seals (Tower), 2 Hen. VI. File 7.*]

December 13th 1423 941. Warrant for safe conduct till 30th April to Sir James of Douglas of Dalkieth or his heir, John   of Seton lord of Seton or his heir, Sir Robert Logan and Sir William Rorthwen knights, to come to the prescence of the K. of Scotland at the city of Durham. Westminster.

Also for John abbot of Balmurynach, Thomas Somervile of Carnwyth, Sir John Forester knight, and Master Patrick of Houston, , **James de Lawedre**[2] of Scotland, William earl of Angus, Adam of Hebborne of Halys [Hailes], Thomas of Hay of Yestyr, Sir William of Abernethy, William of Crychtoun lord of Crychtoun, with 24 persons.
Similar for the Earl of Levenax, Duncan Cambel of Argyle, John Sympyl of Elyotiston, and Robert   of Lille knight of Doughale, to come to the K. of Scotland. *Ibid.* [*Privy Seals (Tower), 2 Hen. VI. File 7.*]

February 3rd 1424 942. Safe conduct under letters patent till the last day of April next for Sir James of Douglas of Dalkethe knight, or his heir, John of Seton lord of Seton, or his heir, Sir Robert Logan and Sir William Rothwin knights, to meet James K. of Scots in the city of Durham, with horses and harness   and servants to the number of 20 persons in all, as hostages for his deliverance. Westminster.

Similar letters patent for the following for the same period:- [the Earl] of Levenaux, Duncan Cambel of Argyle, John Sempyl of Eliotiston, Robert de Lille [Lisle] knight of Doughale - with 16 persons; Archibald de Douglas earl of Wigton; Harbart de Maxwelle of Carlafrok, Harbart de Herys of Tarreglys, John Steward of Dundonnalde, John Steward of Blute (Bute), John Kennedy of Carryk - with 25 persons; the Earl of Morrawe, James de Dunbarre of Frendrauth, Hugh Frysale of Lovet - with 16 persons; John de

---

[2] James de Lawedre, Justice-Clerk South of Forth.

Mongomery knight of Ardrossan, or his heir, Thomas Boyd of Kilmernok, Robert of [Cunyngham] of Kilmauris, Patrick de Dunbar knight of Cunak, James de Hamylton of Cadzow, Hugh Cambel of Loudon (?), John Maxwelle of Calderwood (?) - to the number of 25 persons; Alexander Lyndsay earl of Crawfurd or his elder son, Sir John Lyoun knight, John of   Lyndesay of Birys (?), Andrew Gray of Fauyls, Sir Robert de Levynston knight, David de Lesle lord of Lesle, Norman de Lesle of [Fytherkil, Alexander] of Forbas knight [Alexander of Seton] lord of   [Gordone] - with . . . . persons; [John] abbot of Balmurynach (?), [Thomas] de Somervile of Carnwayth, John [Forester] knight, Walter Ogilvy, Master Patrick of Houston - with . . . . persons; George earl of the March of Scotland, Walter de Halyburtoun lord of Dryltoun [Dirleton], **Robert de Lawedre of Basse knight** - with 18 (?) persons; the Earl of Orkeneye [a cross marked opposite this name], James de Douglas of Balvany, Alexander de Levynston of Calendar - with 24 persons; William de Hay [a cross marked opposite this name], constable of Scotland, or his heir, Robert of Kethe knight, mareshal of Scotland or his heir - with 16 persons; Robert de Erskyn [a cross marked opposite this name], lord of Erskyn, Robert Steward of Lorne, Malcolm Flemyn of Bygare, James of Sandilandis of Calder - with 20 persons; William earl of Angus, Adam of Hebborne of Halys, Thomas Hay of Yestyr, William of Abbirnethe knight, William de Crychton lord of Crychton - with 24 persons; Malice of Grame [a cross marked opposite this name], earl of Stratheryn, Alexander Steward of Fyffe, David Steward *senior*, or the son and heir of the Earl of Athol, John de Drummond of Cargyl knight, John de Wemys of Rerys knight - with 25 persons; **James de Lawedre of Scotland - with 4 persons**; William Olyfaunt lord of Abirdawgy, William de Erthe knight, Alexander de Ramsay lord of Dalwose, William de Borthwick lord of Heriot - with 20 persons. [*Privy Seals (Tower), 2 Hen. VI. File 2.*]

In very bad condition; some names illegible, and others doubtful. A similar conduct of date 13th December previous is on the *Rotuli Scocie*.

February 4th 1424 943. Warrant to the Chancellor for safe conducts to Walter bishop of Brechin, **Edward of Lawedre archdeacon of Lothian**, and Thomas Grenlaw archdeacon of . . . . to pass from Flanders to Scotland; the bishop with 12, and the archdeacons with 8 servants, and horses. Westminster. [*Privy Seals (Tower), 2 Hen. VI. File 2.*]

June 8th 1424 962. Warrant for safe conducts for a year to Walter bishop of Brechin, John abbot of Balmurynach, Sir John Forrester knight, Walter of Ogilvy esquire, **Master Alexander of Lawedre archdeacon of   Dunkeld**, and **Master Edward of Lawedre archdeacon of Lothian**, with 40 attendants, to go to Flanders. Westminster.
Similar for Wautier Clerk and Laurence of Ballochyn, master of two vessels belonging to James K. of Scots, to trade to Bordeaux. Westminster.
Similar for Master Thomas of Myrton of Scotland, with 8 attendants, to go to the court of Rome. Westminster. [*Privy Seals (Tower), 2 Hen VI. File 3.*]

March 4th 1424 976. Similar warrant at the request of the K. of Scotland, to issue safe conduct for half a year for **Robert of Lawedre and Thomas of Lawedre** merchants and burgesses of Edinburgh, to go with two servants, &c. to Bruges and Midelburgh in Seland, to sue for money due to the K.'s said cousin of Scotland. Westminster. [*Privy Seals (Tower), 3 Hen. VI. File 4.*]

June 9th 1425 979. Warrant for safe conduct till Easter next, for Henry bishop of Aberdeen, William bishop of Dunblane, John abbot of Melros, James prior of St Andrew, John abbot of Balmurynach, William of   Borthwick *junior*, and William of Hay knights, Master Thomas of Myreton, **Master Edward of Laweadre**[1] , and Master John Stenes, the K. of Scots' ambassadors setting out for the court of Rome, with 50 attendants. Westminster. [*Privy Seals (Tower), 3 Hen. VI. File 1.*]

---

[1] The Archdeacon of Lothian.

December 4th 1425 988. Warrant to the K.'s cousin the Bishop of Winchester, for a safe conduct till Michaelmas next to Master John Cranok bishop of Caithness, Master James of Hawdenston prior of St Andrew, Master Thomas of Mirton dean of Glasgow, and **Master Alexander of Lawedre archdeacon of Dunkeld**, [later Bishop] ambassadors of the K. of Scots, about to set forth with 50 servants and horses to the Roman court. Westminster. [*Privy Seals (Tower), 4 Hen. VI File 3.*]

January 16th 1431 1042. Warrant for safe conduct for three months for **Master Alexander of Lawedre[2] clerk of Scotland**, presently in Flanders, with his four Scots servants, to pass through England to Scotland.   Westminster. [*Privy Seals (Tower), 9 Hen. VI. File 1.*]

June 25th 1435 1081. Warrant to the Chancellor for safe conduct for two months for **Master Alexander Lawder[3]** and six attendants to pass from Scotland through England to the General Council at Basle. Westminster. [*Privy Seals (Tower), 13 Hen. VI. File 2.*]

Nov. 23rd 1438 1133. Warrant for safe conduct for three months from their arrival at Calais or in England, for **Master Alexander Lawedre[4] clerk**, and David Kennedy (Kendy) esquire, of Scotland, with six ?   Westminster. [*Privy Seals (Tower),18 Hen. VI. File 11.*]

June 28th 1446 1188. Warrant to the Chancellor to issue safe conduct for a year for **William of Lawedre of Halton[1]** with six companions, to come and go once or oftener between England and Scotland. Westminster. [*Privy Seals (Tower), 24 Hen. VI. File 4.*]

---

[2] This is the Archdeacon, later Bishop of Dunkeld (died 1440).
[3] *ibid.*
[4] *ibid.*
[1] Killed at the siege of Haltoun in 1452.

November 9th 1450 1229. Warrant for safe conduct for three years for William earl of Douglas, Sir James of Douglas knight, Sir James Hamylton knight, Sir John Ogilvy knight, [Sir Alexander] Hume knight, Sir William of Cranston knight, Sir Nicholas Cambell knight, Master Adam Auchenlyk clerk, Andrew Grey, **William Lauther**[2] , Thomas [Cranston], Andrew Karre, Charles of Murray, George Haliburton, John of Haliburton, John Doddes, John Grenlawe, George Felawe, **Alan of Lauther**[3] , and James Bysshop, to pass through England to the Marches of Calais and elsewhere in the K.'s dominions, with 80 persons in company. If any fall sick the conduct to endure till his recovery and for twenty days thereafter, to permit his return. Westminster. [*Privy Seals (Tower), 29 Hen. VI. File 5.*]

April 23rd 1451 1232. Warrant to the Chancellor for a safe conduct for 'on hoole yere' to William earl Dowglas as in a bill enclosed, with 100 persons, certain 'herein specified', viz., Sir James of Dowglas knight, Archibald of Dowglas earl of Murrawe, Hewe of Dowglas earl of Ormond, Sir Alexander Hume of that Ilk knight, James lord Hamylton knight, Sir William Meldrum knight, **William of Lawdre of Halton**, Thomas of Cranstone of that Ilk, Andrew Ker of Aldtoneburn, James of Dowglas of Ralston knight, Alane of Cathcart (Kerthkert) of that Ilk, David Hume knight, John Rosse knight, George of Hoppringill, William Balye, George of Haliburton, Marc of Haliburton, **Alane of Lawdre**, Charles of Murrafe, Thomas Bell, Thomas Grahame, James of Dunbar, Robert Heris, William Grerson, John the Menzeis, James of Dowglas, John of Haliburton, Maister Adam of Auchinlek, Maister John Clerc, Thomas Ker, James Ker. [No enclosure.] Westminster. [*Privy Seals (Tower), 29 Hen. VI. File 2.*]

August 14th 1451 1239. Indenture between(eight) commissioners for England, and Thomas bishop of Whithern, Andrew abbot of Melros, the king's confessor and treasurer of Scotland, Andrew lord le Gray, John of Meffen doctor of decrees, Alexander Hume knight, and Alexander Napar esquire, for Scotland, concluding a truce between the

---

[2] of Haltoun.
[3] Alan of that Ilk, younger brother of Sir Robert Lauder of the Bass (d. 1451).

kingdoms for three years from 'sunrise' on 15th August current. Twenty-three (named) consevators of the truce for England, and thirty for Scotland :- William earl of Douglas, George earl of Angus, John earl of Ross, Archibald earl of Moray, Alexander earl of Crawfurde, William lord Creightoun, William lord St Clair, William lord Somerveill, Herbert lord Maxwell, Alexander lord Montgomery, Andrew [lord le Gray, Patrick Hep]burn of Haylis, James of Crichtoun, barons; Alexander sherriff of Angus, Andrew sherriff of Fife, Simon of Glendynwyn, Archibald of Douglas, William of Cranstoun, Walter Scot, Robert of Crichtoun, Alexander Hume, David Hume, Alexander Ramsay knights, James Ru[thyrfurd], Nicholas R[uthyrfurd, Thomas of Cranstoun], William of Carlile, William of Douglas, Adam of Jonstoun, **William Lawedre[4]** , and the admirals, &c. Done in St Nicholas church, Newcastle. [*Chapter House (Scots Docts.), Box 92, No. 16.*]

Circa **June 14th 1464** 1346. Petition for safe conduct for a year to Sir Alexander Forstar lord of Corstorphine, **Sir John of Lawidir of Hawton[5]** [Haltoun] knights, Henry Leberton of the Lainy, John of Wardlawe of Recardton, and Gilbert Forstar, Scottyshmen, with 30 persons of same nation in company, to come on pilgrimage to St Thomas of Canterbury and St John of Amiens (Amyace.) (Granted at Middlilham on 14th June.) [*Privy Seals (Tower), Edw. IV. File 6.*]

November 13th 1470 1388. Warrant to George archbishop of York, chancellor, for a safe conduct for one year to **Robert Lauder** esquire[6], William Roger esquire, and Alexander Preston clerk, of the realm of Scotland, with 16 attendants, to come and go between England and Scotland. Palace of Westminster. [*Privy Seals (Tower), 49 Hen. VI. File 2.*]

---

[4] As note 1.
[5] Although described as "of Haltoun" (technically correct) this Sir John lived on the Burngrange estate at Lauder.
[6] Later Sir Robert Lauder of the Bass (d.c1508), husband of Isobel Hay of the Yester family. His sister Katherine married Sir John Swinton of that Ilk in November 1475.

February 2nd 1477   1445.   James K. of Scots signifies to the bearers of the instalment of the Princess Cecilia's dower due at Candlemas, that he has sent Alexander lord Hume, **Robert of Lawdir of Edrington son[1] and heir apparent to Robert of Lawdir of the Bass,** and Adam of Blackadder (Blacathathir) of that Ilk, with 'Lyon' king of arms, to conduct them to Edinburgh.   Edinburgh.   [*Chapter House (Scots Docts.), Box 92, No. 9.*]

---

[1] Edrington Castle was traditionally held by the eldest son of Lauder & Bass.

APPENDIX III - BIOGRAPHY OF SIR HARRY LAUDER, Knight Bachelor, (1870-1950).

Born Henry Lauder in Portobello, Edinburgh, on the 4th August 1870, the eldest son of John Currie Lauder (1851-1882), a Master Potter and china designer, and Isabella Urquhart MacLeod MacLennan (1854-1905) whose family came from the Black Isle in Rossshire, where her grandfather was a farm manager. Harry's grandfather, also John (d.1888), owned a large house at 4 Rose Street, Edinburgh, which site is now covered by the rear of *Jenners* famous department store. Harry's great-grandfather, George Lauder (d.1824), held the farm of Inverleith Mains (part of which is today the Royal Botanical Gardens) as well as owning the St.Bernard's Well property at Stockbridge, Edinburgh, purchased from the bankrupt Raeburns. They were descended from the Lauder of The Bass family, whose lands at Morham, East Lothian they, as family, were farming until after 1700 by which time they had become tenants following the demise of the senior Bass line.

In 1891 Harry married Ann (1873-1927), eldest child of James Limerick Vallance (1855-1936) a Colliery Manager, and Mary Kerr (1856-1937).

He became a Scottish entertainer of tremendous popularity who toured the world extensively including 22 times to the USA and several times to Australia. Sir Winston Churchill referred to him as "Scotland's greatest ever ambassador". Sir Harry was the first British entertainer to sell a million records.

He became an extensive landowner in Argyll (the Glenbranter estate) and in Lanarkshire.

He was a favourite of King Edward VII, and an intimate friend of Sir Thomas Lipton, the tea magnate, who mentions him several times in his autobiography.

A robust patriot, **Harry raised huge sums of money for war charities during the Great War (1914-1918) and entertained the troops in the trenches in France, where he came under fire.** He was knighted in January 1919 by King George V.
He again entertained troops, and broadcast over the wireless with the BBC Scottish Symphony Orchestra during World War II.

Sir Harry wrote most of his own songs, favourites of which were: *Roamin' In the Gloamin', I Love a Lassie, A Wee deoch-an-doris,* and *Keep Right on to the End of the Road,* and starred in three British feature films: *Huntingtower* (1928) *Auld Lang Syne* (1929) and *The End of the Road* (1936).

He also wrote a number of books which ran into several editions, including: *Harry Lauder at Home and On Tour (1912), A Minstrel In France (1918), Roamin' in the Gloamin'* (1927 autobiography), *My Best Scotch Stories* (1929), *Wee Drappies* (1931), and *Ticklin' Talks* (c.1932). Sir Harry mentions his descent from the Lauders of Lauder and Bass in his autobiography.

His only child, Captain John Lauder (b.1892) was educated at the City of London School, and Jesus College Cambridge where he graduated in Law, then also taking a second degree in music. **John was tragically killed in France 28th Sept 1916 while serving with the 8th Argyll & Sutherland Highlanders.** He was unmarried. Ten years later Sir Harry's wife also died and was laid to rest in the private graveyard at their Glenbranter estate in Argyll.

Sir Harry Lauder died at Lauder Hall, Strathaven, Lanarkshire, on the 26th February 1950. At his funeral service the lesson was read by the Duke of Hamilton and all shops and businesses in Hamilton closed for the day. Sir Harry was interred with his mother at Bent Cemetery, Hamilton, after that town's most memorable funeral ever. It was covered by *Pathe News* and wreaths were received from all over the world, including one from Queen Elizabeth (later the Queen Mother) and another from Mr. & Mrs Winston Churchill.

APPENDIX IV

SCOTTISH DUKES, MARQUESSES & EARLS.
CREATIONS *AFTER* THE UNION OF CROWNS, 1603

Earl of Abercorn	cr. 10/7/160	for James Hamilton
Earl of Aberdeen	cr. 30/11/1682	for Sir George Gordon
Earl of Aboyne	cr. 10/9/1660	for Charles Gordon
Earl of Airlie	cr. 214/1639	for James Ogilvy
Earl of Airth	cr. 21/1/1633	for William Graham
Earl of Ancram Ferniehirst	cr. 24/6/1633	for Sir Robert Ker of
Marquess of Angus	cr. June 1633	for William Douglas
Earl of Annandale	cr. 13/3/1624	for John Murray
Marquess of Annandale	cr. 24/6/1701	for William Johnston
Earl of Athol	cr. 1712/1629	for John Murray
Marquess of Athol	cr. 7/2/1676	for John Murray
Duke of Athol	cr. 30/6/1703	for John Murray
Earl of Balcarres	cr. 9/1/1651	for Alexander Lindsay
Earl of Breadalbane & Holland	cr. 13/8/1681	for John Campbell
Earl of Buccleuch	cr. 16/3/1619	for Walter Scott
Earl of Bute	cr. 14/4/1703	for James Stewart
Earl of Callander	cr. 6/101641	for James Livingstone
Earl of Carnwath	cr. 21/4/1639	for Robert Dalzell
Marquess of Clydesdale	cr. 12/4/1643	for Hamilton
Earl of Cromarty MacKenzie	cr. 1/1/1703	for George
Earl of Dalhousie	cr. 29/6/1633	for William Ramsay
Earl of Dalkeith	cr. 2014/1663	for Scott
Marquess of Douglas 11th Earl of Angus	cr. June 1633	for William Douglas,

Duke of Douglas	cr. 10/8/1703	for Archibald Douglas
Earl of Drumlanrig	cr. 11/2/1682	for William Douglas
Earl of Dumfries	cr. 12/6/1633	for William Crichton
Earl of Dunbar	cr. 3/7/1605	for George Home
Earl of Dumbarton	cr. 9/3/1675	for George Douglas
Earl of Dundonald	cr. 12/5/1669	for William Cochrane
Earl of Dunfermline	cr. 4/3/1605	for Alexander Seton
Earl of Dunmore	cr. 16/8/1686	for Lord Ch.Murray
Earl of Dysart	cr. 3/8/1643	for William Murray
Earl of Elgin	cr. 21/6/1633	for Thomas Bruce
Earl of Findlater	cr. 20/2/1638	for James Ogilvy
Earl of Forfar	cr. 2/10/1661	for Archibald Douglas
Earl of Galloway	cr. 19/9/1623	for Alexander Stewart
Duke of Gordon	cr. 1/11/1684	for George Gordon
Earl of Haddington	cr. 17/8/1627	for Thomas Hamilton
Duke of Hamilton	cr. 12/4/1643	for James Hamilton
Earl of Home	cr. 4/3/1605	for Alexander Home
Earl of Kellie	cr. 12/3/1619	for Thomas Erskine
Earl of Kelso	cr. 25/4/1707	
Earl of Kilmarnoch	cr. 17/8/1661	for William Boyd
Earl of Kincardine	cr. 26/12/1647	for Sir Edward Bruce
Earl of Kinghorn	cr. 10/7/1606	for Patrick Lyon
Earl of Kinnoull	cr. 25/5/1633	for George Hay
Earl of Lanark	cr. 31/3/1639	for William Hamilton
Earl of Lauderdale	cr. 14/3/1624	for John Maitland
Duke of Lauderdale of above)	cr. 26/5/1672	for John Maitland (son
Earl of Leven	cr. 11/10/1641	for Alexander Leslie
Earl of Lindsay	cr. 8/5/1633	for John Lindsay
Earl of Lothian	cr. 10/7/1606	for Mark Kern
Marquess of Lothian	cr. 23/6/1701	for Robert Kerr
Earl of Loudoun	cr. 12/5/1633	for Sir John Campbell
Marquess of March	cr. 26/5/1672	for John Maitland
Earl of March	cr. 20/4/1697	for William Douglas
Earl of Marchmont Lord Polwarth	cr. 23/4/1697	for Patrick Hume,
Earl of Melfort	cr. 12/6/1686	for John Drummond

Earl of Melrose	cr. 20/3/1619	for Thomas Hamilton
Earl of Melville	cr. 8/4/1690	for George Melville
Earl of Middleton	cr. 1/10/1660	for John Middleton
Earl of Newburgh	cr. 31/12/1660	for James Livingstone
Earl of Nithsdale Maxwell	cr. 29/8/1620	for Robert, Lord
Earl of Northesk	cr. 25/10/1666	for John Carnegie
Earl of Orkney	cr. 3/1/1696	for George Hamilton
Earl of Panmure	cr. 3/8/1646	for Patrick Maule
Earl of Perth	cr. 4/3/1605	for James Drummond
Earl of Partmore	cr. 13/4/1703	for David Colyear
Earl of Queensbury	cr. 13/6/1633	for William Douglas
Marquess of Queensbury (grandson)	cr. 11/2/1682	for William Douglas
Duke of Queensbury	cr. 13/6/1684	for Marquess, above
Earl of Rosebery Primrose	cr. 10/4/1703	for Archibald
Earl of Roxburgh Roxburgh	cr. 18/9/1616	for Robert Ker, Lord
Duke of Roxburgh	cr. 25/4/1707	for John Ker
Earl of Ruglen	cr. 15/4/1697	for John Hamilton
Earl of Seafield	cr. 24/6/1701	for James Ogilvy
Earl of Seeforth	cr. 3/12/1623	for Colin McKenzie
Earl of Selkirk Douglas	cr. 4/8/1646	for Lord William
Earl of Solway	cr. 17/6/1706	for Charles Douglas
Earl of Southesk	cr. 22/6/1633	for David Carnegie
Earl of Stair	cr. 8/4/1703	for John Dalrymple
Earl of Stirling	cr. 14/6/1633	for William Alexander
Earl of Strathmore & Kinghorn	cr. 1/7/1677	for Patrick Lyon
Earl of Trequair	cr. 23/6/1633	for John Stewart
Earl of Tweeddale Yester	cr. 1/12/1646	for John, Lord Hay of
Marquess of Tweeddale (son)	cr:17/12/1694	for John, Lord Hay

Earl of Wemyss	cr:2516/1633	for John, Lord
Wemyss of Elcho		
Earl of Wigtown	cr:19/3/1606	for John Fleming

Some titles are older than the above creations, having, at some stage, reverted to the Crown for reissue.

APPENDIX V

The Bass Rock or island [1] lies one mile off North Berwick.
Edrington [1] is near Foulden in Berwickshire.
Tyninghame [1] is south of North Berwick.
Muircleugh [1] is off Lauder common.
Swinton [4] is 6 miles south of Duns, Berwickshire.
Cranstoun [4] is just north of Pathhead, Midlothian.
Polwarth [4] seat of the Homes, is between Greenlaw and Duns,
Berwickshire.
Yester Castle [4] is near Gifford in East Lothian.
Waughton Castle [4] is near East Linton in East Lothian.
St.Germains [1] is near Seton, on the Firth of Forth.
Craigmillar Castle [4] is on the south-eastern outskirts of Edinburgh.
Haltoun [Hatton] [1] is near Ratho in West Lothian.
Belhaven & West Barns [1] are near Dunbar.
Beilmouth [1]: the Beil water empties into the North Sea above
Dunbar.
Gunsgreen [1] is at Eyemouth in Berwickshire.
Whitslaid [1] is two miles south of Lauder.
Popill [1] is in the Parish of Whittinghame, in the Lammermuir Hills.
Dryburgh Abbey [3] is near St. Boswells in Roxburghshire.
Mertoun [1] is near St. Boswells.
Congalton [1] is two miles south of North Berwick.
Newbyggyng [1] is two miles north of Lauder on the Leader Water.
Brownisfelde [Bruntisfield] [1] was in Edinburgh, near the Meadow
Park.
Lasswade [1] is near Loanhead and Polton, west of Dalkeith.
Pirn [2] & [3] is in Peebleshire.
Fountainhall [1] is near Wester Pencaitland, in East Lothian.
Relugas [1]&[4] is in Morayshire.
The Grange Manor & estate [4][1] was between Newington,
Blackford Hill and Nether Liberton in South Edinburgh.
The Ancient Manor was demolished in 1936. A block of flats now
occupies its site.
Johnstonburn [4] is near Haddington in East Lothian.
Ayton Castle [4] is in Berwickshire.

Oxenfoord Castle [4] is near Pathhead, Midlothian.
Burngrange [1] is astride the Lauder Burn at Lauder.
Carolside [1] is three miles south of Lauder (sold to James Home, early 19th Century)
Blythe [1] is 5 miles east of Lauder.
Thirlestane [3] & [4] is 3 miles south-east of Lauder.(Not to be confused with the old Lauder fort on the Leader Water which is now called Thirlestane Castle).
Restalrig [3] is in eastern Edinburgh.
Over-Newton [1] is in West Lothian.
Gogar [1] is west of Corstorphine, West Lothian.
Hawthornden Castle [3] is on the River North Esk, north of Roslin, Midlothian.

KEY:

[1] = Barony or lands possessed by the Lauders.
[2] = Family member had a residence there.
[3] = Family associated with.
[4] = A Lauder married a spouse from family who possessed.

INDEX

Page numbers in italics are illustrations and those followed by n are notes

204

212

214

216

218

Printed in Poland
by Amazon Fulfillment
Poland Sp. z o.o., Wrocław

51094724R00130